YOUR BABY'S MIND
AND HOW IT GROWS

Books by Mary Ann Spencer Pulaski

YOUR BABY'S MIND AND HOW IT GROWS

UNDERSTANDING PIAGET

STEP-BY-STEP GUIDE TO CORRECT ENGLISH

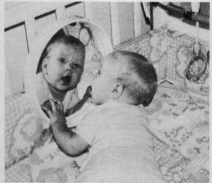
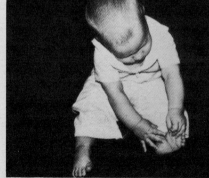

YOUR BABY'S MIND AND HOW IT GROWS

Piaget's Theory for Parents

Mary Ann Spencer Pulaski, Ph.D.

HARPER COLOPHON BOOKS
Harper & Row, Publishers
New York, Cambridge, Philadelphia, San Francisco
London, Mexico City, São Paulo, Sydney

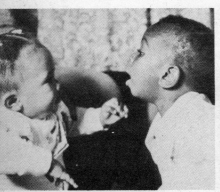

Grateful acknowledgment is given for the following:

International Universities Press, Inc., and Delachaux &
Niestle, Neuchâtel, Switzerland, for *The Origins of
Intelligence in Children,* by Jean Piaget.

Routledge & Kegan Paul, Ltd., and W. W. Norton & Company, Inc., for
Play, Dreams and Imitation in Childhood, by Jean Piaget.
Translated by C. Gattegno and F. M. Hodgson, with the permission
of W. W. Norton & Company, Inc. Copyright © 1962 by
W. W. Norton & Company, Inc.

Routledge & Kegan Paul, Ltd., and Basic Books, Inc., Publishers,
For *The Construction of Reality in the Child,* by Jean Piaget.
Translated from the French by Margaret Cook, © 1954 by
Basic Books Inc., Publishers, New York.

Picture credits appear on page 210.

A hardcover edition of this book is published by Harper & Row, Publishers.

First HARPER COLOPHON edition published 1981.

ISBN: 0-06-090886-6   (previously ISBN: 0-06-013461-5)

81 82 83 84 85 10 9 8 7 6 5 4 3 2 1

To my grandsons
CHRISTOPHER *and* JEFFREY
and to their parents

Contents

Foreword

There have been many changes during the four years of vacations and summers it has taken to write this book. My first grandchild, who inspired it, has grown from an infant to a sturdy kindergartner and now has a two-year-old brother. Mothers have been going to work in droves, and seeking new solutions to the problems of child care. Research is beginning to appear based on single-parent families and on fathers as homemakers. The emerging science of neurometrics is helping us to peer inside the baby's brain and learn how it functions. All of these developments influence babies and our understanding of them. But the way that children's minds grow has not changed very much in the fifty years since Piaget began his observations.

In writing this book I have had the help of numerous parents who have let me share in their children's development. Many of them have taken the delightful snapshots that appear throughout the book; their names are listed on page 210. I am particularly grateful to three professional photographers—Michele Roosevelt, John Hall, and Holly Payne—who spent long hours trying to capture on film some facet of a baby's discovery of his world. Michael Gross of Port Photo Supplies has given me much technical advice, as well as having taken the pictures for the back cover.

I am also very grateful to professional friends who have read this manuscript and offered valuable criticisms and suggestions. They include Dr. Millie Almy of the University of California, Dr. Ruth Formanek of Hofstra University, and Dr. Constance Kamii of the University of Illinois. Mrs. Toni Liebman, director of the Roslyn Trinity Cooperative Day School, gave me much help with the last chapter. Pediatric nurse Ellen Scharf answered my many questions about the newborn. Dr. Judith Kestenberg, a psychoanalyst, shared with me many of her insights into the development of small children. And while the interpretations of Dr. Margaret Mahler's work are my own, I am much indebted to her and her colleagues, Mrs. Anni Bergman, Dr. Fred Pine, and Dr. Ernst Abelin. I owe much to Prof. Selma Fraiberg, too.

My greatest debt, of course, is to Prof. Jean Piaget. Although he is now retired, I was privileged to meet him and attend his seminar during a sabbatical leave spent at the University of Geneva. His associates at the École de Psychologie et des Sciences de l'Éducation accorded me every courtesy. Prof. Bärbel Inhelder and Prof. Hermine Sinclair were particularly kind and helpful, as were Prof. Marianne Denis and Prof. Germaine Duparc. M. Pierre Nicole, who supervises the Jean Piaget Archives, went out of his way to assist me. Dr. Gilbert Voyat, a close friend of Piaget now teaching at City College in New York, relayed many questions to him for me, and helped me translate certain troublesome French expressions. I thank them, one and all.

My very special appreciation goes to my editor, Mrs. Ann Harris, and her associates at Harper & Row. How many editors would spend two hours on Christmas Eve going over the minutiae of a book about to go to press? I am fortunate that she has always been able to help me work through the rough spots with wit and good humor. I am grateful also to Mrs. Rita O'Toole, who typed my much-amended manuscript, and to my family and friends who proofread it and bore with me through long summers of hard work. I hope the result justifies all their help and encouragement.

M.A.P.

March 1978

YOUR BABY'S MIND
AND HOW IT GROWS

What This Book Is All About

This is a book about babies; about how they grow and respond intelligently to the world around them. The human mind at work is wonderful to watch, and in babies we have a chance to observe intellectual growth from the very beginning.

The man who has pioneered in the study of cognitive development in children is a brilliant Swiss psychologist named Jean Piaget. For over half a century, at the University of Geneva, he has been doing research based on his observations of babies and children. In the 1920s, when children were generally regarded as miniature adults, Piaget pointed out that the workings of a child's mind are quite different from ours. A young child perceives the world from a limited perspective, and it is only as he matures mentally and has many and varied experiences with his environment that he comes to think in the logical way that we take for granted.

This development in logical thinking takes place in stages through which every child passes in the same orderly progression as he does through physical stages (i.e., sitting, standing, walking).

The parents and teachers who understand these stages can deal much more effectively with young children and save themselves —and their charges—a lot of grief. I remember the incident of a four-year-old boy who was kicking and screaming in his high chair because his mother, who had forgotten to buy milk, could give him only half a glassful for his supper. Over the noise of his temper tantrum his harassed mother was yelling at him to stop crying and drink his milk when the boy's older sister, a college student, walked into the room.

"It's all right," she told her little brother. "I'll fix it for you."

She took his half-filled glass of milk out to the kitchen and poured the contents into a small juice glass, so that it was filled to the top. Then she took it back and placed it before the sniffling child. He beamed at her through his tears.

"That's what I wanted," he said, "a full glass of milk!" The mother was astonished. To her, half a cup was half a cup, whether served in a juice or a water glass. But her daughter, fresh from a course in Piaget's theories, knew that the four-year-old's judgment was based not on logic but on appearances. If the glass *looked* full, it must contain more than the glass that looked only half full.

This is just one of the many penetrating insights into how children think that Piaget has developed into a body of theory. In America we are only now coming to a wide appreciation of his contributions; his work has been well known for many years in England and France. Piaget writes in French and uses very difficult technical terms, so that even translated into English his work is not easy to read. Nevertheless it is so revealing in its understanding and so rich in its applications that it has influenced child-rearing practices, education, curriculum planning, psychology, psychiatry, logic, and philosophy in many countries.

Piaget, now in his eighties, was originally trained as a biologist. As a child, he was interested in birds, shells, and fossils; he published scientific papers from the time he was only ten years old.

After receiving his doctorate from the University of Neuchâtel in the old Swiss city where he was born, Piaget became interested in psychology, psychiatry, and the study of the mind. He went to Paris to study at the Sorbonne, where he learned to give clinical interviews to patients at a mental hospital. He later became famous for his use of this "méthode clinique" with children, in which he asked open-ended questions like "What do you think of that?" in order to explore the children's ideas. Then he began working in what had been Alfred Binet's laboratory in a public school. His assignment was to give tests of reasoning to Parisian children in order to standardize items for the early Binet intelligence test.

In the course of this work Piaget became very much interested in why children could not reason logically when they were young, but later on could solve the same problems easily. One of the problems he posed was: "Some of the flowers in my bouquet are buttercups. Does my bouquet contain (1) all yellow flowers; (2) some yellow flowers; (3) no yellow flowers?" He found that young children had great difficulty with this question because they could not deal with part-whole relationships. Almost always they gave what were considered "wrong" answers, which Piaget came to realize were part of the developmental process leading eventually to "right" answers. As they grew older, the children could understand the relationship of the part (yellow flowers) to the whole (bouquet).

Observations like this led Piaget to study the reasoning processes of children and to publish his findings in three articles on the development of thought. In 1921 he was offered the position of director of research at the Jean Jacques Rousseau Institute in Geneva. This was a school for the scientific study of the child and the training of teachers; it later became part of the University of Geneva. Attached to it was a little nursery school called the Maison des Petits, where Piaget, at the age of twenty-five, took up what was to become his life's work. He would set up a problem or an experiment for the children and then ask them, "What do you think will happen?" The answers amazed him, for he found that young children had all sorts of magical, emotionally laden ideas about the world around them. He began to record the questions asked by the nursery school youngsters and repeated them to other children, asking, "What do you think?" He learned that a marble rolls down a slope "because it knows you're waiting for it," and that the sun and the moon follow children to "watch over them" or to "keep them warm." In short, he learned that young children see the world and all its natural phenomena in terms of their own experiences and emotional needs. Only very gradually do they change their ideas to conform with objective reality.

During the next ten years the young biologist, now become a psychologist, published five books based on his work with children. These brought him worldwide attention and made him famous before he was thirty. He married one of his students at the Institute, and in time they had three children: Jacqueline, Lucienne, and Laurent. With his wife's help, Piaget studied their cognitive development in minute detail and later published his findings in his landmark book *The Origins of Intelligence in Children.*

It was to this book that I turned and returned many times when I became a grandmother. For years I have been using Piaget's theory to help me understand the children I work with as a psychologist in the public schools. But when my daughter had her two little boys I became an intimate observer of infant development. For me it was an amazing experience to see in them the same indications of unfolding intelligence that Piaget had described in his children a generation earlier. His theories, so new and revolutionary then, have since been tried out by researchers all around the world, and have stood the test of time. With an understanding of mental development in Piaget's terms, baby-watching becomes a fascinating business. The newborn infant is seen not as a sleepy, semiconscious lump needing only to be fed and changed, but as a complex, responsive organism struggling to comprehend and control a bewildering environment.

This book has been written in order to share with all caregiving adults—parents, grandparents, students, teachers, and babysitters—the mysteries and delights of watching a baby's mind grow. I refer frequently in these pages to my grandsons Christopher and Jeffrey as modern American counterparts of Piaget's Swiss children. To them and to many other babies I have known I am grateful for much of the material in this book. But chiefly I am indebted to Professor Jean Piaget, who taught me how to observe and what to look for.

Piaget calls the first two years of life the *sensory-motor* period because the baby learns about the world gradually through his senses and through the motor activities of his body. When he is born the infant cannot distinguish between himself and the world around him because he knows nothing of it. He is, says Piaget, "locked in egocentrism," conscious of nothing but himself. He is not even familiar with the extensions of his own body, as shown by the gradual discovery of his hands and, later on, his feet. The center of the world is his tummy, which is either contracting in hunger or blissfully full. His first organ of learning is his mouth. Through it he learns about the world "out there," about warm, sweet breast milk or flexible rubber nipples, or whatever else finds its way into his omnivorous little maw. He begins to make his first vague classifications: there are things which can be sucked and will relieve hunger (breast, bottle) and other things which can be sucked but do not nourish (thumb, blanket, pacifier). Soon he will learn that there are things which should not be sucked at all. This will constitute a new classification of "no-no's"; gradually he will attach this verbal label to them as he hears Mother saying it whenever she rescues scissors or a safety pin from his grasp. But this process takes the best part of two years, during which time the child effects what Piaget calls "a miniature Copernican revolution." From being conscious of nothing but himself, the center of his own universe, the baby gradually moves to the realization that he is only a part of a larger family and a much larger world. This is no small achievement.

Piaget divides this first period of the child's life into six stages to which he has roughly assigned chronological ages. You will notice that there is a good deal of overlap in these stages, since the ages at which they are reached may differ considerably from one baby to another. Different cultures and environments also show different rates of development; French-speaking children in chilly Canada develop more rapidly than French-speaking children on the relaxed Caribbean island of Martinique. Like the ragged edges of waves on a beach, development proceeds irregularly on many fronts. Each stage, says Piaget, "is the fulfillment of something begun in a previous one and the beginning of something that will lead on to the next."

Piaget never intended that parents should expect their babies to achieve every development within the exact age range that he gives. Now that he has shown us what to look for, we may see some of these developments even earlier than Piaget did. Every baby develops a little differently; some babies may achieve eye-hand coordination early, but be slow to imitate. What *is* important about the stages is their sequence, with the achievements of each stage laying the groundwork for the next one in a hierarchical relationship. The work of many researchers supports Piaget's contention that the stages follow each other in the same general progression. Just as a baby will crawl before he walks, and walk before he runs, so his cognitive achievements tend to follow one another in a predictable order. In fact, physical and intellectual growth are very closely interrelated during the sensory-motor period. As the baby becomes capable of more advanced physical activity, we see him exploring and experimenting further afield. He drops and pulls his toys, opens drawers and climbs stairs, or pokes his fingers into electric plugs and other interesting crevices. Piaget calls this "practical" intelligence, directed at getting results and information from the environment. Gradually, as the child approaches his second birthday, we observe the emergence of clearly mental functions such as memory, imagination, and language. Looking through Piaget's eyes, we can see the baby learning right from birth about his body, the world around him, and how to make it work for him.

In this book we will follow the baby's growth up to the age of three. This will take us through the sensory-motor period and on into the period in which *representation* characterizes the mental activity of the preschool child. The term *representation* refers to the child's growing ability to recognize and imitate and eventually to remember and talk about things which are not directly present to his senses. Well before he is two a baby imitates others and recognizes pictures of familiar objects and people. Between two and three he may try to make his own representations in drawings. The nightmares characteristic of two-year-olds indicate the presence of dreams or "pictures in the head." Make-believe play is another form of representation; a child pushing a block and making siren noises is obviously using the block as a symbol for a fire engine. In learning to talk, the child must use sound symbols which in no way look or feel or smell like the objects or actions they represent. According to Piaget, language develops only after a child has a body of inner images and representations that exist, however fleetingly, long before they can be described in words. Images, memories, and eventually language all evolve and are organized by the child's developing intelligence.

Gradually the child's activity revolves less and less around concrete things present to his senses (sensory-motor period) and more and more around things he thinks about in his head. Piaget uses the term *operations* to differentiate mental activity from physical activity. Thus the period from about two to about six or seven is called the *preoperational* or prelogical period. The child is beginning to think, but his thinking is still about representations rather than abstractions. His perception of the world is based on appearances rather than on logical deductions, as we saw in the example of the little boy with half a glass of milk. This is a very long and interesting period in which the child is struggling to understand the world and how it works. Piaget became famous for his early explorations of the child's view of the world; he pointed out how limited experience and egocentric emotions combine to create distorted and highly personalized explanations of natural phenomena. We shall cover the earliest of these developments in Chapter 7, on the third year of life. All of Piaget's periods of cognitive development are summarized in Appendix A.

Piaget writes comparatively little about the child's emotional development, although he certainly does not deny or overlook the importance of feelings. He says that every intelligent act is accompanied by feelings such as interest or pleasure, and that these feelings provide the energy that sparks intellectual growth. There are many interesting parallels between Piaget's thinking and psychoanalytic theory, but he has preferred to focus on the study of how human beings acquire knowledge, and leave the study of emotional development to others. In this book, therefore, I have supplemented Piaget's work with the theories of child psychoanalysts, primarily Dr. Margaret Mahler and her associates Fred Pine and Anni Bergman. In *The Psychological Birth of the Human Infant*, they describe the slowly unfolding development of the baby as he becomes an individual separate from his mother. For almost twenty years they conducted an informal play center in New York City where mothers came with their babies, and the staff observed the children's day-to-day growth from infancy to age three. The insights yielded by these meticulous, long-range studies of children help us to understand the normal steps in emotional development, which occurs in such close conjunction with intellectual development.

Mahler and her associates point out that a baby is physically born at a clearly delineated point in time, but that his psychological birth takes much longer. It is a "slowly unfolding intrapsychic process" that continues during the first three years of life. The infant in his egocentrism experiences himself as still a part of his mother; he does not begin to recognize her as a distinct individual until around six months of age. It takes another two and a half years before the child is a fully separated individual with a sense of his own identity.

This long process of individuation and separation from the mother is not complete until around the end of the third year, the period of time covered by this book. I have included a discussion of the child's emotional development along with each chapter on intellectual development so that the two can be considered as complementary aspects of the same growth process.

In each chapter there is also a section on toys and games appropriate to that age level. However, children's play, particularly the make-believe play characteristic of two- and three-year-olds, is such an important topic that it is covered more fully in a separate chapter that follows the stages of development. There is also a separate chapter on language, which may appear at widely varying ages; it, too, has its own characteristic pattern of development. I would suggest that if you are reading this book while watching a particular baby grow, you should skip ahead to Chapters 8 and 9 after you have read Chapter 3, since the beginnings of language and play both emerge in the second year.

It is with considerable regret that I have been forced to fall back on the usual sexist pronouns *he* and *she* in writing this book. I did experiment with alternatives, but none were acceptable.

Rather than struggle with the awkward *he or she* construction, I have used *he* to refer to babies in general, and *she* to refer to the primary caregivers. May the feminist movement forgive me and may there soon be a suitable nonsexual alternative!

This brings me to a subject which has given me deep concern during all my work on this book. There is a revolution in child care going on in this country, the outcome of which no one can yet predict. Young mothers are going back to work in droves; close to 40 percent of the mothers of preschool children are already working, with the greatest increase in numbers coming from the mothers of children under three. Of this group, 33.8 percent, or more than a third, were working by March of 1976. The Women's Bureau of the United States Department of Labor projects that between 1975 and 1985 there will be a 32 percent increase in the number of working mothers with preschool children.

This means that if the trend continues—and there is every reason to believe that it will—by 1985 close to half of the nation's babies will be cared for by mother substitutes. Women are breaking new ground every day in employment areas previously restricted to men, and the women's movement is heartily encouraging them. The women who are free to meet these challenges have my full support and admiration, but young mothers must face the question, "What about the babies? Who is taking care of them?"

The answers are many and diverse—relatives, babysitters, nursery schools, day care centers. Fathers, when they are present, are becoming increasingly involved; and some are the primary caregivers for their babies. At the same time great numbers of fathers are leaving the home, and as the divorce rate climbs, thousands of children are being raised in single-parent families. These phenomena—the young working mother, the father as "househusband," the single-parent family—are all so recent that we have little research or knowledge about their effects or implications. We cannot say how good or harmful they may be in the long run, or how they will affect the development of the babies experiencing them. We know very little about what happens to babies who are raised primarily by their fathers or by sitters or in day nurseries, largely because it is almost impossible to generalize about any one of these situations. There have been no systematic long-term studies taking into account the many variables involved: the age of the child when the mother goes to work, how long she is absent, how she feels about her job, the attitude of the baby's father (if he is in the home), and the quality and consistency of the substitute mothering the baby receives. These are among the many issues that have yet to be investigated in depth.

The research which is presently available, however, is based largely on children in traditional family settings. From this large body of literature, as well as from generations of experience, we know that babies need consistent, loving care from a stable central figure. Classically, this has been the mother; if she is gone much of the day, there has to be someone who is a warm, familiar substitute. In these pages you will see how the baby's intelligence unfolds in response to a safe and stimulating environment. All of Piaget's observations of infants were made in such a home, while most of the follow-up studies were based on children raised in traditional family settings. Mahler's research, while it took place in a children's center, used frequent, long-term observations of normal mother-child pairs. I have deliberately avoided as much as possible the literature on emotional deprivation as observed in institutionalized children, but even in normal children there are clearly recognizable phases in cognitive and emotional growth which call for support and understanding from at least one consistent, affectionate adult. For the purposes of this book, I have called that person "the mother"; conceivably it could be the father, the grandmother, or a truly involved babysitter. For it is not just the experience of giving birth which makes a person a mother, but the whole process of caring for a baby's needs and feeling oneself needed. The full experience of motherhood can only be understood by a "mothering" person.

Most often this relationship develops between infants and their mothers, so there is an unspoken assumption in these pages to which the reader is asked to adjust. If you are a father, read "parent" instead of "mother." If you are a young mother away at work, remind yourself to ask your baby's caregiver about the developmental milestones described in these pages. When your baby discovers his toes or searches for a hidden object, she may notice sooner than you do.

In any case, the purpose of this book is to help all caring adults understand the day-to-day development of a baby's mind. For parents, it is designed so that you can make the most of your time with your child, whether you are at home all day or only for a few hours. I sometimes wonder whether young mothers who are "bored silly" or "climbing the walls" really know how fascinating their babies are. Watching the infant from a Piagetian perspective, we can see his growing intelligence reflected in the ways in which he responds to his surroundings, and eventually reaches out and takes control of them. If we understand how the world looks to the very young child, we can help him deal with anger and frustration; we can answer his questions appropriately for his age, and even re-ask them of him as Piaget did, in a way that will tell us more about his needs.

Each one of us is shaped by feelings and experiences we cannot remember. Yet the way we were treated in our earliest months and years may affect our lifelong feelings about ourselves and the way we treat our own children. If we want them to grow up alert, inquisitive, and unafraid, we must provide an environment that is both safe and stimulating. Then we must sit back and watch them discover the world and construct their understanding of how it works for themselves. For babies do not learn by being either pressured or overprotected. Nor is it enough to surround them with the latest "educational" toys and then ignore them. Babies learn best by exploring and experimenting, each in his own way, watched over by loving parents who are wise enough to understand what they are learning. This is the wisdom of Piaget that I would like to pass on to you.

CHAPTER 1

The Very Beginning

Stage One—Birth to 1 Month

At the time Piaget began his research, newborn babies were considered helpless, passive organisms, insensitive even to painful stimulation. Piaget drew attention to the competence of the infant, and to his responsiveness to light, sound, movement, touch, and taste. In the past fifteen or twenty years there has been an explosion of research about the newborn which shows that he is an active, attentive, selective little being who is perceiving and organizing a myriad of sensations from his earliest days. He can discriminate smells and tastes, and will turn away from strange odors but will seek out the smell of his mother's breast milk. During the first week of life he may respond to such sounds as a rattle, a bell, or pure tones of different pitches. He may sleep better if he hears a rhythmic sound pattern that reminds him of his mother's steady heart beat *in utero*. Very early he will look toward the sound of a soft, high voice, particulary his mother's. He will often startle and cry if touched with something cold like a metal disk, and give strong indications of feeling pain when pricked.

The eyes of the newborn will open wide in a dim light, and he may look toward its source, particularly if it is moving. Researchers have found that newborns cannot focus beyond eight or nine inches from their eyes, and their eye movements are uneven and jerky. In less than a week, however, they can discriminate between two patterns displayed just above their cribs, and will look longer at black and white patterns than at colored surfaces. Longest of all they will gaze at the human face, particularly the eyes. Because babies are dependent upon human beings for their survival, this appears to be a highly adaptive response that is innate in the newborn.

According to Piaget, the beginnings of intelligence lie in just such adaptive responses. The baby is born into this world equipped with certain innate, uncoordinated reflexes such as sucking, swallowing, grasping, and crying. Primitive though they may be, these are the building blocks of intelligent behavior. For Piaget the biologist as well as Piaget the psychologist, *"intelligence is adaptation."* Just as he had once watched snails in the rough waters of Lake Neuchâtel change their shape in order to

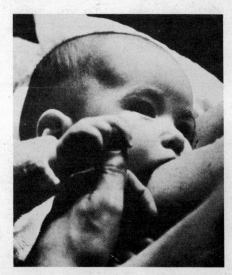

get a better hold on the rocks, so Piaget watched his infants organize and coordinate their reflexive responses to meet new environmental situations.

Take sucking, for example. Every infant is born with a sucking reflex, but it varies greatly from one to another. Some babies are fussy nibblers; some are hungry guzzlers. They may have to adapt to bottles with different kinds of nipples held in different ways by different parents. Each mother is individual in the size and shape of her breasts and in her manner of nursing. The infant may have to cope with tiny, underdeveloped nipples, or heavy breasts that threaten to smother him, or with a mother who holds him too tightly or too carelessly. Mahler describes a woman with long, pendulous breasts who laid her baby across her knees and simply leaned over him, so that her hands were free.

Babies have to adapt to all these variations and many more. The ways in which they do it differ with the individual infant. Some newborns have a hard time finding and holding onto the nipple. They may root around, sucking the skin of the mother's breast in the wrong places. Others quickly learn to find the spot that brings them satisfaction and nourishment. Piaget noted that his son Laurent seized the nipple with his lips on the second day of life, without having to have it held in his mouth to stimulate him.

In so doing, Laurent was carrying out the two processes which Piaget says go on continuously during all intelligent, adaptive functioning. He was adjusting his body, his head, and his lips so as to find his mother's nipple, and thus he was *accommodating* himself to the external reality of her body. At the same time he was taking in or *assimilating* nourishment and stimulation for himself. We shall meet these two processes many times at many levels of adaptation as the child grows older. Here we see them at their biological beginning in the infant's life. Piaget noted that from birth Laurent would lie in his crib, making sucking movements with his lips and turning his head slightly from side to side

—an instinctive sucking and rooting behavior, even when the breast was not available. Within a half hour of birth he accidentally got his hand to his mouth and began to suck it. By the third day he began to suck the moment his lips touched the breast, groping for the nipple until he found it. Already Laurent was refining his previously undifferentiated rooting and sucking reflexes to achieve more effective results—and in the process he was learning his first lessons about the location of objects (the nipple) in space. Soon he learned to turn his head immediately to the side on which he felt the breast against his cheek. Long before he knew left from right he was beginning to develop a sense of laterality (sidedness) and direction.

By the ninth day Laurent's sucking response had become generalized to other objects. Piaget observed that in his searching he knocked against a quilt and a wool coverlet in his crib. He sucked each of them for a moment, and then began to cry. At three weeks he found his thumb and sucked it; he also sucked Piaget's index finger. When he was placed near the breast, however, he would search for it in what appeared to be a truly purposeful way. Piaget noted with interest that when Laurent was not hungry he would suck on fingers or quilts, but when he was hungry he would stop sucking them and cry until nursed. This illustrates the beginning of discrimination: in other words, the dawn of intelligent behavior.

It also illustrates the modifiability of reflex actions. Each time he was nursed, Laurent grew a little more efficient in coordinating all the elements of the nursing situation—finding the nipple, grasping it, sucking, and swallowing. Gradually he organized his actions into a stable, integrated, oft-repeated unit of behavior which Piaget calls a *schema*. At the same time that he was assimilating his mother's milk more smoothly, Laurent was accommodating to her body, adjusting to her position and to the side she preferred. A mutual process of adaptation was taking

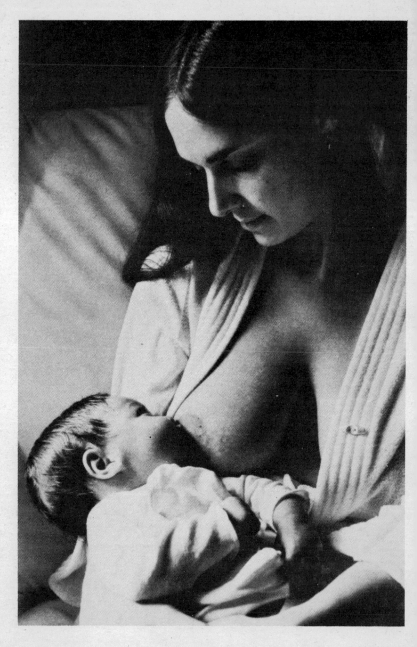

place between mother and child, each giving comfort and pleasure to the other.

Another schema that develops during the nursing situation is that of looking. Many mothers have noticed in the early days of life that their babies seem to focus on their faces during nursing, and literally "devour" them with their eyes. "My baby's really looking at me!" they will say happily when true eye contact begins. This intense looking of the infant serves two purposes. The more he practices focusing on a near object, the better he learns to perceive. And the more he gazes with bright, alert eyes at his mother's face, the more she responds to him—smiling, cooing, talking to him—thus encouraging him to continue his visual exploration of the world. As Dr. Aidan Macfarlane has pointed out, when a mother is holding her newborn her face is about eight or nine inches away, her eyes are looking into his, and she is talking to him in a soft, high voice—all creating an optimal situation for the infant. His reflex responses to her voice, her eyes, and her breast become joined together to form a new and more complex schema of social awareness.

Of course, not all reflexes expand and develop like those we are discussing here. Some, like yawning or sneezing, are already fully organized at birth. Others, like the standing reflex, usually disappear for a while and then reappear later in more mature, voluntary form. Many a new mother gets unduly excited because her baby, if held erect against a solid surface, will stand and even step forward. This ability usually declines in the first six weeks, to reappear at somewhere around four or five months, when the baby is able to support his weight by locking his knees.

The crying reflex is one which is evident at the moment of birth, but is soon modified to fit a variety of situations. An experienced mother can tell from the infant's cry specifically what is troubling him. There is the demanding wail of hunger, the sharp scream of fear or pain, the howl of anger, and the drowsy fussing of the baby who is almost, but not quite, asleep. Some babies cry more vigorously and consistently than others, but all babies cry when they are hungry, cold, startled, or in pain. The pain may be internal, due to anything from a "bubble" to lying in the same position for too long; or it may be external, caused by a soiled diaper or an open safety pin. Some babies cry when bathed; others when they are naked or wet. They will often stop when picked up and gently talked to, or distracted by a bright object moved slowly past their eyes. Toward the end of the first month fussy or "fake" crying may appear, characterized by low moans interspersed with an occasional cry. To most parents this means the baby "wants attention." Listen carefully and you may hear an occasional gurgle or squeal. The baby is experimenting with his first noncrying vocalizations. In succeeding weeks you will hear new sounds such as "pff" or "baaa." It is out of vocal experiments such as these that language eventually develops.

One reflex which has strong emotional significance for parents is the smiling reflex. The first fleeting smiles of infants may occur very soon after birth. Folklore says that they are due to "gas pains," though I have never heard any evidence to support this theory. They frequently occur after feeding, when the infant is drowsy and content. Dr. Peter Wolff of the Boston Children's Hospital has made a special study of these smiles as differentiated from later "social smiles." He considers reflex smiles to be spontaneous ways of discharging energy before falling asleep, since they do not seem to occur when the baby is alert and active. For one month he observed eight newborns, watching them daily in the hospital and for thirty hours a week in their homes. He found that within two to twelve hours after delivery, all eight infants grimaced in a way that suggested smiling. Just the corners of the mouth turned up; the rest of the face was not involved.

Wolff also used a bell, an Audubon bird whistle, and tape

recordings of mothers' voices to get the babies to smile. By the second week they were responding increasingly to high-pitched voices, and also smiling spontaneously after nursing. When the babies had drunk their fill and their eyes were still open but glassy, the turned-up mouth, says Wolff, gave them "a stupid, almost intoxicated appearance" that brought great amusement to their parents. During the third week all eight of the babies gave the first clear indications of a "social smile" in response to a high-pitched voice. They were awake and bright-eyed, and the smiles were broad, crinkling the eyes and involving the whole face. By the end of the fourth week the babies were smiling not only at the voice but at the sight of a smiling face. They seemed to be making eye contact, and mothers who had not played much with their babies before suddenly began to respond to them, saying, "Now he is fun to play with!"

Piaget reported smiling in each of his children during the second month. Dr. Joseph Church, in *Three Babies*, records smiling by two of his three subjects at three to three and a half weeks, and at seven weeks for the third. Even blind babies are said to

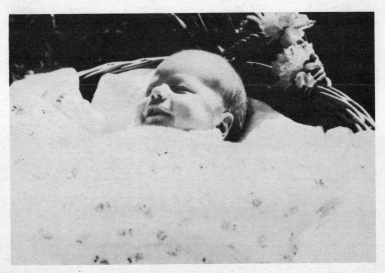

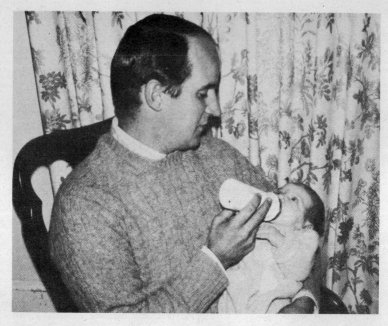

smile by about six to seven weeks. Whenever true smiling comes, it is undoubtedly a landmark in the mother-child relationship. The baby smiles in response to his mother's smile, and she smiles with delight in response to his! Thus the infant's behavior is encouraged and attuned to his particular mother-child relationship. The biological reflex develops into a psychological behavior pattern.

In this mutual smiling response we can see clearly the crucial role that parents play in the psychological and cognitive development of their babies. The reflexes, the hereditary "givens" of behavior, are enough to allow survival, but adaptation and learning come in response to environmental stimulation. We have seen how the sucking reflex, clumsy and fumbling at the start, becomes organized and streamlined until the infant can nurse smoothly and efficiently. When that life-giving activity is consolidated, he has time to look around while he is nursing, and his eyes fix upon his mother's face. Her smiles and soft words feed his sensory needs just as her milk nourishes his body. Soon he begins to smile, not just as a reflex, but in response to the expressiveness of her face. This is the beginning of social behavior.

The father has an important part in this process too, for he provides a different kind of stimulation—the feel of hairy, muscular arms, the tickle of whiskers, a masculine smell, and the sound of a deep voice. The father can bathe or dress the baby or give a bottle very efficiently. Most important of all, he can hold his tiny offspring. Babies require a lot of holding, especially in the evening when they are fussy and mothers are tired. Gentle handling and holding, particularly skin-to-skin, is a warm and wonderful experience for the baby; it stimulates both his neurological and his emotional development.

We know this because of important new advances in monitoring the electrical activity of brainwaves by EEG (electroencephalograph). The results, analyzed by computers, give information about sensory, perceptual, and cognitive processes and the developmental maturity of brain activity. This is a comparatively new branch of neurology from which much is yet to be learned. We know more about the emotional effects of handling babies, both from research done in orphanages and hospitals where babies are deprived of loving attention and from the case studies of psychoanalysts such as Mahler.

The latter agrees with Piaget that the newborn infant is "locked in egocentrism." He is completely self-involved, and much of the time he seems oblivious to everything around him. He is fully occupied with struggling to adapt to this strange new environment. His body must establish regular patterns of breathing, eliminating, and taking in food—all functions which his mother's body took care of during the months of fetal life. The only language he understands is that of touch. Close, secure holding and skin-to-skin contact communicate a sense of safety and being cared for that reassures the startled infant. That is why some obstetricians now place the newly born infant on the mother's warm abdomen to rest after the exhausting experience of birth. Mothers will instinctively pick up a crying baby and hold him close, usually against the left side. Dr. Lee Salk proposes that this is because the baby, when held on the left, has his head resting close to the mother's heart; he has noticed this position in classical paintings as well as in living mothers, both right- and left-handed. His research suggests that babies *in utero* grow used to the pulsating sound of the mother's heartbeat, and find it soothing even after birth.

It is in these intimate moments of holding and feeding that the baby's first learning takes place. That is why it is so important not to ignore the nursing infant, and *never* to simply prop him up with a bottle. For most mothers and babies, this is a very precious private time—one that makes siblings and sometimes fathers a little jealous. One young mother told me that some of her sweet-est memories were of the 2 A.M. feeding when she and her baby were all alone together in a dark and sleeping household.

The baby at this stage is not even aware that his mother has an existence separate from his. Since conception he has always been with her, and in the nursing situation he is blissfully reunited with her warm body, drinking in the sight and sound and smell of her. In time he will begin to recognize her as a separate and very special person in his life; but for now, they are one. His greatest emotional need at this stage is for the reassurance of prompt gratification. So when your baby cries, pick him up, even when you feel he is crying "just for attention." Attention is as important as food at this age, and no mother would deny a baby who is crying "just for food"! Pick him up and hold him close—don't worry about spoiling him yet. Soon enough he will learn that there are times when he must accept frustration and delay. But first he needs your loving to teach him how to love, and to make him feel that the world is a good and reliable place. Too many adults don't know how to give love because they never really received it. They are afraid to make decisions or to take chances because they never learned to feel really safe and secure as babies. It is this sense of "basic trust," as Erik Erikson calls it, that provides the emotional soil in which the baby's intelligence can grow and flourish.

TOYS AND GAMES

There is little that needs to be said about toys for the infant of less than a month old. People are the best toys—loving human beings who hold and nurture him. A comfortable rocking chair can give both parents and child hours of pleasure. There are also swinging cradles which can be wound up to run automatically; about sixty rocks a minute seems to be the most soothing speed. The infant might enjoy brief periods of looking at a psychedelic lamp with kaleidoscopic patterns of changing lights. He is probably oblivious to all the toys his visitors bring him. He may look momentarily at large magazine pictures of human faces taped to the side of his crib, or something like a round Christmas ornament suspended above him. I suggest this because it can be looked at from underneath; most mobiles are meaningless from the infant's point of view. I remember going into my grandson Jeffrey's nursery, where he lay sound asleep under three mobiles of circus animals and nursery rhyme figures which were two-dimensional so that he could scarcely see them. His three-year-old brother Christopher, who could see them sideways, found them enchanting and didn't understand why Jeffrey didn't look at them. The adult who is seeking social responsiveness from an infant at this age can sympathize with Christopher's plaintive question: "Why he still sweepin'? He better get up and pway!"

CHAPTER 2

Discovering Oneself

Stage Two—1 to 4 Months

This is a very pleasant stage, both for your baby and for you. By the time he is six or seven weeks old, your infant is becoming adapted to his new surroundings. Feeding and napping routines are fairly well established, and he may even be sleeping through the night—a welcome change. During the day he is awake and alert for longer periods. He now turns his head in the direction of sounds he hears, and looks for longer periods. He is beginning to coo and blow bubbles with his saliva; soon he will be crowing and gurgling. Most delightful of all, he is beginning to smile! During the next two or three months he is very good company. You can put him in a portable crib and take him out with you at night. He can be passed around among admiring friends and relatives, and the miracle of his sudden smile will melt the hearts of total strangers. Toward the end of this stage he may be chuckling and squealing with laughter when you tickle him or toss him up in the air. He is lots of fun—but he can also dissolve into sudden tears if he becomes overstimulated or tired. Learn to read his body language—the drooping head, the puckering lips—and be sensitive to his needs.

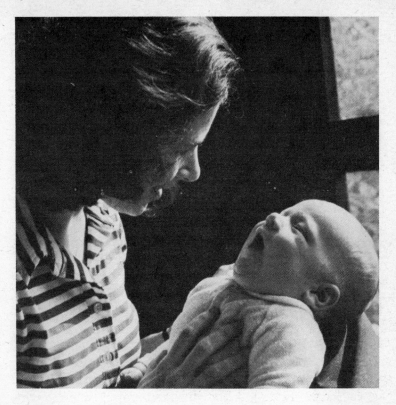

Psychologists call this "the problem of state," and it is very important in dealing with babies. An infant who is hungry or sleepy is in no mood for fun and games. A pediatrician cannot examine him reliably, nor can a photographer get good pictures if he is screaming his head off. Most mothers can "read" their babies pretty well and soon learn what to do to quiet them or perk them up. Picking them up, talking to them gently, giving them something to look at or listen to, can change a fussing, unhappy state to one of alert interest. Conversely, playing games such as those described at the end of this chapter at the wrong time can be overstimulating and exhausting. So learn to be aware of your baby's state—when he wants to play, and when he needs to tune out the world.

Don't leave your baby alone in the crib when he's not asleep; this is a precious opportunity for him to learn from his surroundings. He may enjoy reclining in an infant seat where he can watch you as you move about. You will notice his eyes following you with increasing interest as you talk and sing to him. If he makes a sound and you imitate him, he may stare at you and then try to repeat it. Or you may get him to stick out his tongue or clench his fist as he watches you do it. These are the faint and not very dependable forerunners of imitation, which later on plays an important part in cognitive development.

A playpen is useful at this stage, because it enables the baby to move freely and to watch you in action as you in turn watch him. You can see him energetically exercising his limbs or struggling to roll over. For this is the stage of self-discovery; the baby is slowly learning the limits of his body and what it can do. If you put him on his tummy, his little head bobs up and down as he tries to control it. By the end of this stage he will be able to hold it up straight and look around him for ever longer periods of time.

When your baby is lying on his back, particularly with his diaper off, you can see a human dynamo in action. His arms begin to flail and his legs to kick as rhythmically as if he were pumping a bicycle. Obviously he is enjoying the experience of motor activity, even if he's not sure just what it is that he's activating. We know this from the curious intensity with which he stares at the little fist flying past his eyes. It moves across his gaze like a planet in outer space. He seems to have no control over it, or awareness that it is attached to him. It is only by accident that he gets it into his mouth where he can suck it. Once having enjoyed this experience, he wants to repeat it over and over. During the next few weeks he spends a lot of time watching this wandering hand. Gradually he learns to slow it down, control it, and direct it to his mouth to suck. Only by practicing these activities repeatedly does he finally achieve mastery over them. Then, as Piaget says,

"It is no longer the mouth that seeks the hand, but the hand which reaches for the mouth." The sensory sucking reflex is joined with the motor control of the hand to form a new sensory-motor schema.

This is typical of the adaptive schemas characteristic of the second stage. The baby, in the process of trying to achieve control over his own movements, accidentally produces a new result. He then repeats the same movements over and over, at first in a jerky and uncoordinated way, but eventually with smooth control. Watch him struggling to suck his thumb apart from his other fingers, for example. He is modifying his movements to adapt to new objectives, and thereby expanding his repertoire of behaviors.

Many other adaptive schemas are constructed by the child during this second stage. He learns to look around in response to a sound (hearing coordinated with vision) or to start sucking at the sight of his bottle (vision coordinated with sucking). The latter is an interesting schema because it shows us the dawn of

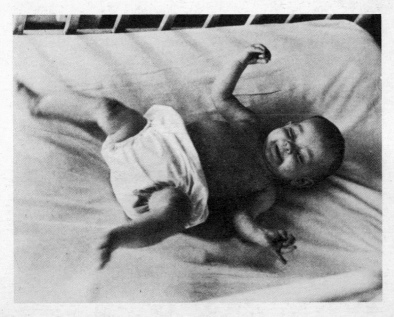

anticipation. The baby now knows what to expect when he sees the bottle, and gets ready to suck even before the nipple touches his lips. But the most important development is that of grasping as it combines with vision to become prehension—visually directed reaching and grasping.

The grasping reflex is apparent at birth. If you pry open the fist of a newborn infant and touch his palm, his tiny fingers will close around yours, but they will soon let go. By the second month the infant can close his hand to fit around an object placed in it well enough to hold it for a few minutes. This is the beginning of accommodation. But when he drops the object, he does not search for it in any way, either with his eyes or with his hand. The infant in his egocentrism is not aware that objects exist outside of his own consciousness. Since he is not even fully aware of the boundaries of his own body, he spends long periods gazing at his waving fists, which appear and disappear from his visual field. Sometimes the hands collide with each other accidentally, and then the infant may try to clap them together again in a repetitive way, but there is no real control of the eyes over the hands.

By the third month the hands begin to open and finger play appears. Piaget describes Lucienne, his younger daughter, watching her right hand open and close. "There is as yet no precise coordination between these movements and sight except that the fingers seem to move more when Lucienne looks at them." Here the baby seems to be developing a primitive kind of visual control over her hand; it moves into her sight by chance, but she tries to maintain and control its activity with her eyes. This is a first step toward visually guided grasping, which does not occur for several weeks yet.

At this point the hand-mouth schema is considerably more developed than is the eye-hand schema. Very early the hand finds its way to the mouth to be sucked; it is also capable of

grasping objects. The next step is for these two reflexes to be joined, so that when the hand grasps something like a rattle, it is brought to the mouth to be sucked. At first this combination of behaviors takes place without the baby's seeing what it is that he is grasping. Whatever he grasps, he sucks; and whatever he sucks, he grasps. The two schemas have become reciprocal, creating a more complex schema of grasping-sucking. Then one day in the course of his random movements, the baby's hand holding a rattle appears before his eyes. We have already noticed how attentively he watches his hands— imagine his interest in this new and exciting spectacle! You may see his whole body quiet down while he concentrates on looking at that little hand. Gradually, with much repetition, he learns to coordinate his kinesthetic and motor activities so that he can control the movements of the rattle across his visual field. A third system has now been assimilated to the previous schema. Soon the eyes will take precedence over the mouth as the principal organ of learning.

Not yet, however; there is more control to be established. So far vision has played no part in the grasping of objects, but has only enjoyed the sight of the hands moving by. The next step comes when an object such as a gold chain is dangled close to the baby's hand, so that both hand and object are seen at the same time. The baby will reach toward the object and eventually will grasp it. This does not happen overnight; it is a complicated coordination of seeing, reaching, swiping, missing, and finally grasping. If either the object or the hand is not in the visual field, there will be no reaching, as shown in the following observation made by Piaget when Lucienne was four and a half months old; note that in Piaget's abbreviations of his subject's age 0;4(15) represents 0 years, 4 months, and 15 days.

Lucienne, at 0;4(15) looks at a rattle with desire, but without extending her hand. I place the rattle near her right hand. As soon as Lucienne sees rattle and hand together, she moves her hand closer to the rattle and finally grasps it. A moment later she is engaged in looking at her hand. I then put the rattle beside her; Lucienne looks at it, then directs her eyes to her hand, then to the rattle again, after which she slowly moves her hand toward the rattle. As soon as she touches it, there is an attempt to grasp it, and finally, success. After this I remove the rattle. Lucienne then looks at her hand. I put the rattle beside her. She looks alternately at her hand and at the rattle, then moves her hand. The latter happens to leave the visual field. Lucienne then grasps a coverlet which she moves toward her mouth. After this her hand goes away haphazardly. As soon as it reappears in the visual field, Lucienne stares at it and then immediately looks at the rattle which has remained motionless. She then looks alternately at hand and rattle after which her hand approaches and grasps it.

It was through hundreds of these precise and painstaking observations that Piaget was able to put together what Dr. Burton
White has called "far and away the most outstanding body of
work we have on human infancy." Watching carefully, Piaget
noted the emergence of ever more integrated, better organized
behavior patterns in many areas of sensory-motor development.
The last step in this particular series is, of course, the complete
coordination of vision and grasping: the baby both looks at whatever he grasps and grasps (or tries to) whatever he sees. This
tendency of babies can make life difficult for parents, but we must
accept it as a natural outgrowth of the coordination of vision and
grasping. When the baby pulls your beard or grabs your earrings,
just remind yourself: it simply means he's learning to direct his
hands more competently!

This schema of prehension (visually directed reaching and
grasping) is important: through it the infant eventually realizes
that the object (i.e., the rattle) is distinct from the action (grasping). The baby is becoming dimly aware that there is a world of
things "out there" that exist separately from his body and his
actions upon them. This is the first crack in his shell of egocentrism. The Copernican revolution has begun! However, most of
the repetitive activities of Stage 2 center on the baby's own body
and are not directed at objects in his environment until the end
of this stage. As we have said, the infant stumbles upon a new
sensory-motor experience as a result of something he does quite
accidentally. He then repeats his movements over and over in a
kind of rhythmic cycle until he has perfected a new schema. I
knew a baby girl who at two months used to scratch everything
—her covers, her face, her mother's breast. It became her preferred way of responding to her environment.

What brings about all these new developments in the baby?
For one thing, his motor control and his visual apparatus are

maturing rapidly. For another, his brain is beginning to take control of his body. You can actually see the change during these months, as brain functioning emerges. There are fewer stereotyped, machinelike reflexes and more responses centrally controlled by the brain, which coordinates both sides of the body. These include "bicycling" with all four limbs, or bringing both hands together at the body's midline. Recent research suggests that there is indeed a critical turning point in neurological maturation at around three months which is tied to significant changes in perceptual and learning capabilities. The infant can now hear about as well as an adult, and can perceive patterns as a qualitative whole rather than as a series of parts. By the end of the fourth month he can focus his eyes on close or distant targets as flexibly as the average adult. He can follow objects moving either horizontally or vertically without the jerky eye movements of the newborn. This means he is ready for new and more interesting sights. You may notice him staring at the pattern on his curtains, or scratching at the flowered print on your blouse. Your baby is telling you that it's time to move his crib to a different perspective, put up a new mobile, or change the pictures on the wall. Having nothing interesting to look at may cause him to become fussy or drowsy. As one researcher put it, "We have found that the infant actively seeks out stimulation, attends selectively, and given an opportunity to control his stimulus environment, he demonstrates a vigorous appetite for stimulus change."

In other words, during this stage the baby begins to show distinct needs and preferences. Part of this is due to heredity; babies are born with very different endowments and temperaments, as every parent knows. But the environment plays an equally important part in the development of personality and learning styles. Active babies demand more stimulation and attention, and usually get it (unless their mothers are ill or overburdened). A quiet, passive baby may need the stimulation more, but may not get it because he lies contentedly, sucking his hands, gazing around, and exploring his fingers. This is not necessarily bad; he may be assimilating a great deal and consolidating it more fully than his more vigorous peer. But if adults around the passive baby are aware of this tendency, they can make a special effort to pick him up more often and give him the extra cuddling and stimulation that will encourage him on the road to learning.

Other environmental factors, such as position in the family or the season of birth, can affect a baby's learning rate. First babies get more adult attention, but younger ones learn a great deal from their siblings. Christopher, racing around with his red hair flying, was a human mobile who constantly entertained Jeffrey at this stage. Piaget describes many interactions between his children which show how Jacqueline drew little Lucienne into her activities. He also points out the effect of seasons on a baby's learning. Lucienne and Laurent, he says, watched their hands moving when they were two months old, whereas Jacqueline, his firstborn, did not accomplish this until a month later. His explanation was that the younger two were born in the late spring and were much more active and unfettered, while Jacqueline was born in January and spent most of her days outdoors on a balcony, well bundled up. Consequently, Piaget confesses, he spent much less time experimenting with Jacqueline than with Lucienne or Laurent, with whom he was "constantly busy." In the endless controversies over the effects of heredity versus environment, Piaget is an interactionist; he has always believed that the baby's inherited characteristics interact from birth with the particular environment into which he is born to produce his individual personality.

Modern research strongly supports this interactionist point of view. The work of such psychologists as J. McV. Hunt and Burton White has shown that changes in the environment can speed up cognitive development if they come at the right time for the baby. Dr. White of Harvard worked with institutionalized infants who spent their first four months in plain white cribs lined up in the nursery of a state hospital. White blankets, hung over the sides to protect the babies, cut off any glimpses of the outside world. Busy nurses fed and bathed them but had no time for cuddling or playing. The infants just lay there on soft mattresses which sagged so that even rolling over was difficult.

Dr. White chose a group of six-day-old infants for his study of visually directed grasping. First he got a nurse to give each baby twenty minutes a day of extra handling and stimulation. After a month of this he changed the babies' flat white world by giving them gaily designed, colorful sheets and crib bumpers. Each crib got an interesting stabile with shiny balls and rattles on it. The mattresses were firmed, and babies were placed on their tummies after daytime feedings, with the bumpers removed so they could rear their heads and watch the activities in the ward. For some of the babies this was just too much enrichment; they did a lot of crying and looked less frequently at their hands than did the unaffected control group. By two and a half months, however, they were able to adapt to all this stimulation and showed real enjoyment—looking around them, taking swipes at the stabiles, smiling and burbling happily. They were the noisiest, most active group in the nursery!

This experiment illustrates what psychologist J. McV. Hunt calls "the problem of match." If there is too much stimulation the infant simply cannot assimilate it all; either he ignores it or becomes distressed, as White's babies did at the beginning. When he is a little older he is ready for more experience and takes to it joyfully. Since older babies prefer novel and complex stimuli, while young infants prefer simple, familiar ones, we must always match the level of stimulation to the child's level of maturity. Too little is boring; too much is overwhelming.

With this in mind, White selected a new group of infants. After the first month of extra handling, he gave them a transi-

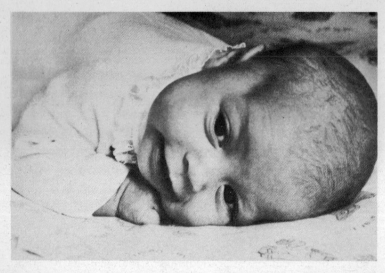

tional month with only two bright red and white targets to look at. Then at two and a half months he placed them in the colorful environment already described, and watched them respond. These children did the best of the three groups, showing heightened interest in looking at their surroundings, and learning to reach for objects almost eight weeks sooner than did the babies in the control group who received no extra stimulation.

It is interesting to note, however, that the control group, reared in the usual bland institutional surroundings, learned to watch their hands at about the same time as the experimental babies did. As Piaget has suggested, all children learn sooner or later, and if we rush them, we do no good and only create tensions. Watch your particular baby, and when he seems restless and bored, give him something new and interesting to attend to. Not only will he enjoy it, but he will slowly become more and more aware of you as the source of comfort and pleasure.

The emergence of this dim awareness of the mother marks the beginning of what Mahler calls *symbiosis* (a Greek term meaning "a living together"). In this stage the infant "behaves and functions as though he and his mother were an omnipotent system—a dual unity with one common boundary. . . . [It is a] state of undifferentiation, of fusion with the mother in which the 'I' is not differentiated from the 'not-I' and in which inside and outside are only gradually coming to be sensed as different."

What this means is that the infant in his egocentrism assumes that his mother is a part of himself. Out of this "dual unity" develops his capacity to respond to other people and things in the world—indeed, to know that the world exists. Only during the course of many weeks does the infant come vaguely to perceive in his mother the source of his need satisfaction. As she bathes, changes, feeds, and plays with him, he begins to sort out the sensations on the outside of his body from those at its core. He hears sounds around him, and sees faces which at first appear and disappear as if he were seeing them, to quote Piaget, "through the windows of a moving train." But slowly they stabilize and consolidate until the baby begins quite early to recognize his mother's face, then those of other members of his family. At around six to

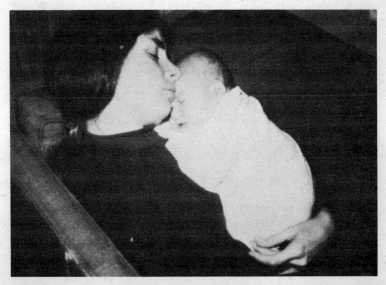

eight months the baby can differentiate familiar faces from those of strangers. At this stage, however, the baby responds to any human face, as we can tell by his joyous and indiscriminate smiling.

Another aspect of this dual unity is the "omnipotent system" to which Mahler refers. Since the mother has the power to comfort and satisfy her infant's every need, and since she exists only as part of him, it follows that her power is really *his* power. He feels that he commands her, and she does his bidding. He cries; she comes. He is hungry; she supplies nourishment. He is wet; she makes him comfortable. The good mother gives her child the feeling that his wishes are magically understood and fulfilled; since he knows no better, he thinks the magic emanates from himself. Here begins the feeling of magic omnipotence which pervades childhood and often lingers on in the semiconsciousness of adults. We wish upon a star and hope the wish will come true. But for the baby, wishing is the same as willing, and when his wish does come true, he has a wonderful feeling of magical power which knows no bounds. This is because he has as yet no knowledge of his own limitations.

The role of the father in early infant development is currently the subject of much interest. So far, research indicates that there is no inborn biological preference for the mother, and that the father who is frequently available in the home and who cares for the baby may be recognized almost as early as the mother. If and when fathers become primary caregivers while their wives work, we may see a revolution in attitudes toward the role of the father. Certainly we know that he has an important part in the baby's cognitive and emotional development. He gives a different kind of stimulation, as we have previously noted. He spends more time playing with his child, rather than performing mundane tasks like feeding or bathing. It is quite probable that from the baby's point of view, Mother means business, but Father means fun!

TOYS AND GAMES

You do not have to spend a lot of money on toys, because right in your own home you have a rich variety of interesting things with which to entertain your baby when he is ready. Since at this stage everything goes into his mouth, you must make sure that what you give him is nonpoisonous (if painted) and safe to suck. A set of sturdy plastic measuring spoons is colorful and harmless and makes interesting noises. Watch your baby accommodate his mouth to their different sizes and shapes. Well-sanded wooden

clothespins (not the spring variety) are easy to hold and fit in the mouth. A bangle bracelet of bright enamel or plastic is fun to look at and suck. When teeth are coming through, a silver spoon feels cool against swollen gums, particularly if it has been left in the freezer for a little while. An ice cube feels good, too, but don't let go of it in the baby's mouth because he might choke on it.

For mobiles, you can make bright balls of stuffed flannel and hang them from a ribbon tied securely across the baby's crib. Watch him swipe at them with his hands or feet and set them swinging. One of these days he'll discover the cause-and-effect relationship between his actions and the movement of the balls.

Whether you buy rattles or receive them as gifts, examine them carefully for safety—more than one baby has nearly choked on them. You may prefer to spend your money on a musical mobile or a wind chime to hang outside the window. A silver bell is lovely if it's safe to handle, but beware of clappers that can come loose and be swallowed. A colorful pinwheel securely tied to the hood

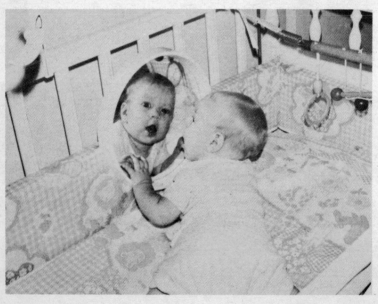

of the baby's carriage will delight his eyes when he's outside. For Christopher I bought one of those huge plastic sunflowers that people put in their gardens. He used to lie in his playpen under the trees in the summertime and watch it rotate in the wind.

Infants begin to get very interested in their own images as they try to define the limits of their bodies. Try hanging a safe, sturdy mirror against the inside of your baby's crib, and watch him peer into it and smile at himself. A floor-length mirror will draw his attention all through the first year or so. Put your baby in front of it in his infant seat and let him study his reflection. At first he will just stare at it, looking puzzled. Later he may get very excited and flail his arms wildly, gurgling with pleasure. But in the beginning he is content just to look at himself, slowly building a recognition of what he sees.

There are a number of games you can play with your baby that will entertain him and tell you how well he is developing. Sit him in his infant seat and hold a bright object about ten inches in front of his eyes. When you are sure he is looking at it, move it around him in an arc of 180 degrees. Watch to see how well he tracks it. Repeat this several times and see if his eyes linger at the point where the object disappears behind his chair.

When your baby has mastered this game, try passing the object around and behind him so that it reappears on the opposite side. Watch to see how soon he learns to turn his head from the point of its disappearance to the side where it reappears. He probably won't be able to do this until he is about five months old, but when he does, you will know that he is able to anticipate the object's path in space.

As visual prehension develops, your baby will try to reach for the object you hold in front of his face. If he doesn't, move it close to his hand so that he sees them both at the same time. Watch to see whether he tries to grasp the toy, whether he can do it successfully, and how he does it. Does he have to see his hand and the object at the same time? Does he look back and forth from his hand to the object? Does he enjoy these games, or does he get frustrated and start to cry? If so, stop and wait a week or two before trying again. *Never* tease or push the baby beyond what he is able, or almost able, to do. You must match your stimulation to his state and the level of his development.

Imitation games are fun if your baby is responsive. Nod your head, waggle it from side to side, or stick out your tongue. Make noises or imitate your baby's sounds. Clap your hands and see if he makes a move to copy you. Some babies love games like these.

Probably the most fun for babies, however, are the games you play that help him define the limits of his own body. He may enjoy "Peekaboo" although he doesn't really understand it yet. "Pat-a-cake" and "This little piggy went to market" make him aware of his fingers and toes. One game that I learned from an

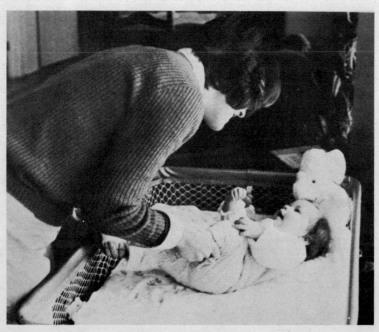

orthopedist years ago, when my son's kicking was not properly synchronized, was to lift his right and left legs up and down alternately in a seesaw motion while reciting this nursery rhyme:

> Seesaw sacaradown,
> Which is the way to London town?
> One foot up, the other down,
> This is the way to London town.

In our family the favorite game, from my childhood to my grandchildren's, is a variation of the tickling game which I will pass on to you. One of my earliest memories is that of my white-bearded grandfather with his deep bass voice. He used to lean over me, his forefinger moving in wide circles which slowly spiraled in on my fat little tummy as he recited sonorously:

> The bumblebee behind the barn
> Carries his bagpipe under his arm,
> And this is what the bumblebee says,
> Bzzzzzzzzzz!

With the "bzzz" he would zoom in to tickle me as I quivered with anticipation. Could there be a more delightful memory of babyhood?

CHAPTER 3

Discovering the World

Stage Three—4 to 8 Months

During the next four or five months you will see tremendous changes in your baby. Life will never be as peaceful again, for now he is becoming mobile. At the beginning of this stage he is probably rolling over and creeping on his belly. Soon he will get his legs up under him and start to crawl on all fours. Most babies can sit up alone by six or seven months, which gives them a whole new perspective. By the eighth month some babies are pulling themselves to an upright position and standing erect, holding onto the furniture.

As each of these skills develops, it increases the baby's mobility and thus enlarges his world. Sitting up, the child can see his legs and feet much more easily. If he hasn't already discovered his toes, he certainly will now. He spends hours on his back, trying to get them into his mouth. When he begins to crawl, he gets under tables and into closets, and learns that things look different from underneath than from on top. He is learning with his body the meaning of "under" and "over" and "inside," and the difference between objects and empty space. These are all spatial con-

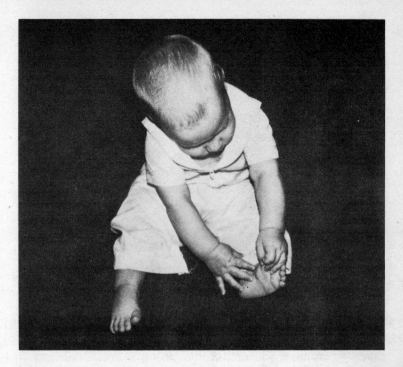

cepts that must be constructed at the sensory-motor level. Long before a child can understand the terms "left" and "right," he must have a million experiences of laterality, or sidedness, and of opposite directions. Through his body he finds out about his environment; this is what Piaget means by "practical" intelligence. It cannot be stressed too often that the infant does not simply take in stimulation from the environment; he *constructs* through his actions a growing knowledge of objects as they exist in the world about him. He learns that some bounce, some roll, and some even break. Thus he comes slowly to comprehend the nature of reality that exists independent of his actions.

Obviously, the more experience he gets, the more opportunity your baby has to assimilate and construct new knowledge. So when you see him beginning to take off by himself, don't plop him in the playpen—let him explore. But first you are going to have to babyproof your home. Put books and precious breakables out of reach, and install gates on the stairs. Get plastic covers for the electric wall outlets and catches to secure low cupboard doors from the inside. You can slip a yardstick through looped drawer handles, or you can keep your bottom drawers filled with interesting nonbreakables for your baby to pull out and investigate. Sweaters and scarves in the bedroom, wooden spoons and plastic containers in the kitchen—they're all new and interesting to him.

Not only is your baby becoming more mobile, he's learning to use his hands more efficiently to touch, hold, turn, shake, and bang. At four or five months he needs both hands to grab an object, and has to drop one toy to pick up another. But soon you will see him transferring objects from one hand to the other, so he can hold one and reach for the second. Around seven months he discovers the lovely crackling sounds of paper, and you will find it is no longer safe to leave magazines or newspapers on a low table. The easiest solution is to give him his own special pile of papers to crumple, squeeze, crush, and rip.

The major achievement of this stage is the adaptation of known, oft-practiced schemas such as these hand movements to new situations. Previously the baby's activities were centered mainly on perfecting these activities themselves: looking in order to see better, grasping in order to suck more, babbling for the satisfaction of hearing his own voice. Now that he is able to direct his body more efficiently, the baby's attention moves outward to things happening in the world around him. It is an almost imperceptible change, easier to recognize when it is past than when it is actually occurring. But if you watch your baby you will notice his eager response to each new experience. He may accidentally bang the slats of his crib, or kick a mobile hanging over it, causing it to flutter. Often he will stop quite still and listen or stare; then he may smile at this unexpected phenomenon. Research has shown that his heartbeat slows down, as if he were reacting with: "Hold everything! What's going on here?" Then he will repeat whatever he has done with renewed vigor, as if trying to prolong this interesting experience. Piaget describes just such a moment:

> Lucienne, at 0:4(27) is lying in her bassinet. I hang a doll over her feet which immediately sets in motion the schema of [shaking]. . . . But her feet reach the doll right away and give it a violent movement which Lucienne surveys with delight. Afterward she looks at her motionless foot for a second, then recommences. There is no visual control of the foot, for the movements are the same when Lucienne only looks at the doll or when I place the doll over her head. On the other hand, the tactile control of the foot is apparent: after the first shakes, Lucienne makes slow foot movements as though to grasp and explore. For instance, when she tries to kick the doll and misses her aim, she begins again very slowly until she succeeds (without seeing her feet).

Here we notice the same repetitive activity that we saw in Stage 2, except that it is more complex and better controlled. Lucienne first kicks the doll by chance; then she tries again, slowly and deliberately. Her kicks are not random but are groping toward the doll, trying to prolong the sight of its swinging. Also—and this is the important development—Lucienne's attention is centered here not on the process of kicking, but upon the doll, something existing in the world outside of her.

You will see this in your baby as he begins to move around the house, exploring cupboards, shelves, and fireplaces, and leaving a trail of disorder behind him. His characteristic procedure, like Lucienne's, may be to shake everything first, as if all things were classified as objects-to-be-shaken, whether or not this schema is appropriate. (Piaget describes Laurent's shaking of a wooden paper knife as if it were a rattle.) He may even discover that there is a relationship between the degree of energy with which a toy is shaken and the amount of noise it produces, as Piaget shows us in this interesting observation of his son.

> In the evening of 0;3(13) Laurent by chance strikes the chain while sucking his fingers: he grasps it and slowly displaces it while looking at the rattles. He then begins to swing it very gently which produces a slight movement of the hanging rattles and an as yet faint sound inside them. Laurent then definitely increases by degrees his own movements: he shakes the chain more and more vigorously and laughs uproariously at the result obtained. On seeing the child's expression it is impossible not to deem this gradation intentional.
>
> At 0;4(21) as well, when he strikes with his hand the toys hanging from his bassinet hood he visibly gradates his movements as a function of the result: at first he strikes gently and then continues more and more strongly, etc.

In these fragments of behavior, Piaget detects the first primitive efforts toward classification based on sensory-motor activity (objects-to-be-shaken or objects-to-be-sucked). He also points out to us the growing awareness of relationships (harder, slower, louder, etc.) between actions and things. These are cognitive concepts which assume growing importance as the child's intelligence develops. We may also be seeing the first faint connections between cause and effect.

In both these observations the children's actions were directed toward repeating new experiences caused by accidental striking or shaking. Piaget calls these actions "procedures to make interesting spectacles last." The baby at this stage is not yet aware of cause and effect as separate entities—all he knows is that his action is in some magical way associated with a pleasing result. He may perform the same action when it is no longer appropriate. For example, he kicks his feet, and the toys in his crib sway. So when he sees the curtains at the windows move in the breeze, he may kick his feet again, as if expecting the curtains to move at his command. In his magic omnipotence he does not separate the result (the movement of the curtains) from the action (his kicking), because he does not yet conceive of the objects which produce these results (the curtains) as existing separately from his actions upon them.

For in spite of the baby's evident interest in the objects around him, his actions suggest that "out of sight is out of mind." True, his eyes have been following moving objects almost since birth, and now if something disappears he may look around for it. But if it is not in view, the child acts as if it no longer exists. He has not yet developed the notion of the permanence of objects in the world around him. In his egocentric experience, objects exist solely as a result of his actions upon them, which include seeing and hearing them. It is only after many experiences with objects that swing or roll or drop out of sight but later reappear, that the baby begins to search for them as if he expected to find them still visible. In the meantime, life is certainly easier for parents who

have only to remove from sight the eyeglasses, fountain pen, or lipstick the baby grabs for.

This "search for the vanished object" develops gradually during Stage 3. Piaget describes hours of dangling his gold watch in front of his children and dropping it into their laps. He noted that first they would look in astonishment at his empty hand—the watch was gone! Then they would look in front of them where the watch might be expected to land; but if they did not see it or feel it at once, they would give up. However, if Piaget lowered the watch slowly enough for their eyes to follow it, or if the chain made an accompanying sound, the children would search for it. Thus the watch took on independent existence only as a result of the child's activity. Piaget tested this further by letting the children do the dropping, and found that "the search for the fallen object takes place more often when it is the child himself who has let it drop. . . . The object still exists only in connection with the action itself."

> At 0;8(20) Jacqueline takes possession of my watch which I offer her while holding the chain in my hand. She examines the watch with great interest, feels it, turns it over, says *apff*, etc. I pull the chain; she feels a resistance and holds it back with force, but ends by letting it go. As she is lying down she does not try to look but holds out her arm, catches the watch again and brings it before her eyes.
>
> I recommence the game; she laughs at the resistance of the watch and still searches without looking. If I pull the object progressively (a little farther each time she has caught it) she searches farther and farther, handling and pulling everything that she encounters. If I pull it back abruptly, she is content to explore the place where the watch departed, touching her bib, her sheet, etc.

From observations like this we get a sense of how very long it takes the growing baby to construct the notion of *object permanence*, Piaget's term for the knowledge that objects outside the infant have an independent existence of their own in space. We adults make inferences about objects so quickly because we have had years and years of experience in dealing with them. For us this is all contained in a single second's judgment; for the baby the process is lengthy and slow. He learns about objects by acting upon them: pushing, poking, rolling, and squeezing. The more freedom he has to explore and manipulate different kinds of objects, the sooner he will assimilate them to his growing body of knowledge. This notion of object permanence takes time to build, but it is the major intellectual achievement of the sensory-motor period, since it enables the baby to differentiate between himself (egocentrism) and external objects in space.

How babies construct their knowledge about external reality is being studied at Yale by two psychologists, William Kessen and Katherine Nelson. They are finding, as Piaget did long ago, that if you want to know what the infant experiences, you must ask the right questions: questions based on *his* point of view, and not on what seems important to adults.

For example, for many years it has been accepted that the earliest discriminations between objects were based on color and shape. But in doing research on the words that children learn first, Kessen and Nelson found that "ball," "dog," and "car" were consistently included in their earliest vocabulary. Since these are all things that move, Kessen and Nelson theorized that "an infant's primary categorization of objects is based on their dynamic properties." To test this hypothesis, the researchers devised experiments in which they put a shape on a mechanical arm and set it in motion in front of the infant. Then they changed the shape but continued the motion; or they changed the direction of the motion but kept the shape the same. They found that babies paid more attention to the changing motion than to the shape. In the same way, they varied color and motion, and came up with the conclusion that motion is more important to infants than either shape or color. In other words, say Kessen and Nelson, infants do not organize the world as adults do. They seem to make "a functional analysis of the world—what is movable, what is eatable, what is touchable." They note that concepts in the child's cognitive system such as "bounceability" or "rollability" are not even recognized in adult language.

This ongoing research demonstrates why it is so important to give babies the freedom to explore and experiment with the world in their own way. We do not always know what their most effective cognitive approaches are. When we insist on showing them "the right way" to stack up blocks or fit shapes into a sorting box, we may be preventing them from making their own discoveries in ways that are more meaningful to them.

During these months babies are learning more about sounds as well as about objects. They are babbling and vocalizing much more expressively now. You may hear repeated syllables such as "mama" or "dada," and your delighted response to these sounds encourages the infant to use them again. (See Chapter 9, on the development of language.) Babies will point at what they want and make very demanding noises. They will turn their heads toward familiar sounds and may even respond to their own names.

At this stage babies will sometimes imitate simple movements which are already familiar to them and which they can watch, such as clapping or making a fist. From time to time there are reports that some babies as young as two or three weeks will imitate an adult's facial gestures such as sticking out the tongue. Babies can also be taught to wave "bye-bye" quite early, but Piaget calls this kind of meaningless gesture *pseudo-imitation*. Babies imitate it only if they are continually encouraged by their parents. One imitative game they *do* seem to enjoy by the end of this stage is "Peekaboo," even though their role may be a passive one. Piaget seems to agree with psychoanalysts who theorize that this game symbolizes the return of the beloved parent.

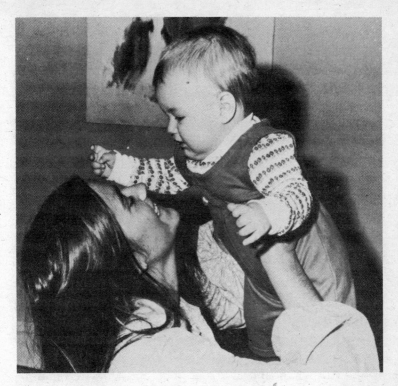

It says to the baby: "I may disappear for a little while, but I always come back." It builds the child's trust in a safe, dependable world, and in the permanence of objects which remain stable whether he sees them or not. His mother, that most important of objects, is the first one *not* out of mind when she's out of sight. Her disappearance may cause him brief anxiety, but he rejoices in the reassurance of her return.

The gradual realization of his separateness from his mother is the first step in what Mahler calls "the psychological birth of the infant." For four or five months he has been safely sheltered within the protective warmth of the symbiotic relationship with his mother. Her body, her breasts, her voice, her smile, and her tender ministrations are so much a part of his experience that he scarcely knows where she ends and he begins. The search for his body boundaries which began in Stage 2 gave him the first clues; now, as he moves to discover the world around him, he slowly becomes aware of his mother as different from other people—in fact, different from *him!* He begins to explore her face and body more actively, pulling her hair or ears, grabbing at her glasses, tweaking her nose, putting his fingers into her mouth and ears. He looks at her carefully, scanning her face and comparing it to the faces of other people. Although he is happiest in her arms, he may twist and turn, trying to study her from different angles.

These signs of differentiation, as Mahler calls this process, show that the infant is slowly becoming aware that he and his mother are separate. And with that awareness comes the emotional need to cling to this very special person who has literally given him life. No longer will the baby respond freely and cheerfully to anyone who wants to hold or smile at him. He prefers to sit in his mother's lap and study strangers for a while.

This means that from about six months on, the visitor who comes only occasionally must adapt his or her approach to the baby's state. Even familiar grandparents and babysitters must be careful not to pick him up too abruptly. Of course, in this as in all ways, babies differ widely. But you would be wise to watch your baby's reactions and suggest to your friends and relatives the most acceptable way to approach him. A guest coming into your home should ignore the baby and just chat with you for a few minutes while the baby sizes up this comparative stranger. It is best not to look at the baby directly or make friendly overtures until he seems relaxed and willing to make eye contact. When a baby returns your gaze, crouch down to his level or sit facing him so you are not towering over him. Then a smile, a few words, or a friendly gesture may be successful. But don't push your luck—the baby may cover his eyes with his hands or burst into tears and bury his face in his mother's shoulder. On the other hand, he may be serious and wary, or very curious and interested in you. It all depends on the particular baby and on his state at that moment. If he has just awakened, he will be much more touchy than if he is wide awake, alert, and ready to face the world.

This aspect of the baby's emotional development usually begins to appear somewhere around six months and reaches a peak at about eight months. It may subside toward the end of the first year but is likely to reappear during the second year and at any stressful times in the young child's life. Certainly it has to be taken into consideration whenever you are leaving your baby in the care of another person or visiting in a strange household. It is a normal part of the baby's growing up, and demonstrates his new cognitive ability to discriminate between the familiar and the unknown, as well as showing his special attachment to you. It may be inconvenient for you to have to cope with a clinging, screaming baby when you are in a hurry to go out, but it will pay big dividends in the future if you can go slowly now and help your baby to accept your absence. Try to leave him with someone he knows and trusts, such as his father or grandparents. If that's not possible, have a familiar babysitter come early and engage him in play for half an hour or so before you leave. Always tell him that you are going out, but that you love him and you will be back soon. Even if he doesn't understand your words, your tone of voice— affectionate, confident, and firm—comes through to him. Don't be gone very long the first few times. If he learns that when you disappear you *always* come back, his basic trust in you will be reinforced and he will separate from you more easily as time goes by.

The baby at this age may be as comfortable with his father as with his mother in the presence of an unfamiliar person. A researcher in Boston made several studies of how young children react when left with either or both parents in a playroom with a stranger. His subjects were about three hundred children from six to twenty-four months old. His major conclusion was that infants and toddlers "do not spontaneously show a unique behavioral response to the mother but respond similarly to fathers and mothers." This supports the observation common to many parents that in families where the father is home early and sees a lot of his child, the baby learns to know and trust his father almost as soon as he knows his mother. When Daddy comes home at night, both mother and baby perk up and respond to his presence.

TOYS AND GAMES

By this age the baby is paying more attention to the decorations in his room. Make it interesting for him, and not only can you stimulate his sensory development, but you may be able to sleep a little later in the morning while he entertains himself. There are delightful prints available for children's curtains and beds; the baby loves to point to the various animals or Raggedy dolls decorating his room. (This may help to keep him still while you struggle with changing his diapers.) Big, colorful posters of children or baby animals are inexpensive enough to be changed every few weeks, and will give your baby something new to look at when he wakes up. As time goes by, you can introduce smaller, more complex figures—even copies of famous masterpieces such as Breughel's *Children's Play* or a lovely Madonna and Child. Hang interesting mobiles of birds or fish or a model plane from the ceiling light fixture and change them periodically.

Toys that promote listening are also interesting to babies. They will fall asleep to a tape of Mother's voice telling a story or singing lullabies. When Christopher was old enough to grab and pull, I got him a plastic bluebird that could be strapped to the railing of his crib. It had a music box inside it which he could start by pulling on a ring. Sometimes at night or early in the morning my daughter would hear the music box playing. Instead of crying, Chris was entertaining himself.

Another favorite crib toy for this age is a cradle gym. Your baby can practice reaching, grasping, and pulling himself up on it. He may like a "busy box,"* but shop carefully, for some are really not suited for babies. Unfortunately, the people who design "educational toys" for children are sometimes more interested in selling to adults. Like the mobiles mentioned in Chapter 1, such toys may be meaningless to children, at least in the age span for which they are recommended. The best way to buy toys is to know your child and his abilities and choose accordingly.

You can now begin to encourage language through the use of very simple picture books. Even at four or five months babies will look at pictures of familiar objects while you name them—a ball, a truck, a kitten. This is a good time to get your child into the cozy habit of sitting on your lap to "read a story" together. Perhaps Daddy can do it while you're getting dinner (or vice versa). In either case, it is a good introduction to the storytelling situation and can be used to teach your baby how to handle books. As we have said, babies at this age love to tear paper, so very heavy cardboard books or cloth books are safest. Christopher's favorite was a discarded textile sample book of my husband's. Made of heavy fiberboard with a spiral binding, it contained a whole line of samples of plastic fabrics ranging from "wet look" vinyl to soft, suedelike foam. Chris sniffed and felt every one of the samples, looked at the color displayed on each page, and eventually learned to point to various colors on request.

The baby will experience a variety of smells, tastes, and textures without any thought on your part—the scent of Mommy's perfume, the tickle of Daddy's beard, the flavors of many foods, the

---

*A box constructed to encourage several different manipulative abilities. It may include a door to open, a buzzer to sound, a wheel to turn, or a mirror to look into. It straps to the railing of the crib or playpen or hooks over the side of the bathtub.

slippery smoothness of soap. But occasionally let him sniff something interesting—fresh mint from the garden or vinegar in a
salad dressing. Give him a taste of your ice cream, a sip of your
soup. Babies are beginning to drink from a cup at about this age,
and like to gum on the edge of a cold glass. Now that teeth are
pushing through, a chicken leg with all meat and bone splinters
removed is delicious to suck and chew on.

When the baby begins to play on the floor, he will enjoy
colorful balls. For the creeper, I recommend a small rubber ball,
about four inches in diameter so that he can see over it. Roll it
gently toward him and he will swipe at it, making it roll away. As
he grows more competent he will reach out into space for it. The
more he reaches out after objects, the more he will realize they
are there. But if the ball rolls out of sight, the baby will probably
stop looking for it.

However, if you hide a toy such as a bunny under a cushion so
that part of it is still visible, you may find your baby going after
it with enthusiasm. This indicates that he has the beginnings of
an image in his mind that enables him to recognize the whole
bunny from just the ears that he now sees sticking out. When he
can succeed at this game, try letting him watch you hide the
bunny under a diaper (or any other light covering). See whether
he searches for it, and if so, whether he succeeds in lifting the
diaper and finding it. These are all steps toward developing a
memory image of the bunny in his mind, even when it is out of
sight.

For these hiding games, use toys the baby is actively playing
with and is eager to keep in sight. If his interest wanes, let *him*
play with the toy or even hide it himself, while you become the
searcher. Remember what Piaget pointed out: at this stage the
object exists only as a result of the child's actions. If your baby
seems uninterested in or frustrated by these games, always stop
and wait for a week or so before trying them again.

When your baby can sit up securely, bath time becomes great fun. Water poured through funnels and strainers changes its form in interesting ways. Filling and emptying different sizes of plastic bottles and jars lays the groundwork for the concept of quantity. An egg beater can be used to make a froth of soapsuds, and turning the handle encourages motor coordination. There are all sorts of commercial bath toys available in addition to what you can adapt from your own household. But whether you buy toys or improvise, you must be alert to all possible dangers to your

child. Before you buy toys, examine them carefully. Tug at the buttons and eyes of dolls and stuffed animals; check the metal whistles on rubber squeeze toys. Examine anything you give a child for sharp points or edges. Wood and plastic should be sturdy enough so that they will not splinter or break. Keep ribbons and cords short enough so that they can't entangle your baby. Watch for rust on metal parts; be sure that all paint is labeled nontoxic and all fabrics are flame-resistant. The Consumer Product Safety Commission does a good job, but it can't check everything. Only you can do that.

In spite of all these warnings, don't be afraid to let your child explore, for that is how he learns. If you hover over him, always worrying about possible dangers, you are communicating to him that the world is a fearful and unsafe place. You are also encouraging him to be dependent on you. So make your home as safe as you can, and then let your creeper go to it! An occasional bump or fall is inevitable, but he'll learn very quickly how the law of gravity works. Hold your breath if you must, but encourage your baby with a smile. He still has worlds to conquer.

CHAPTER 4

The Emergence of Intention

Stage Four—8 to 12 Months

Toward the end of the first year you will find your cuddly, dependent baby transformed into a living dynamo. He is ready to take off on his own, and nothing is out of bounds. He crawls all over the house, around and under the furniture, often resenting the time required to eat or sleep. He pulls himself upright and cruises along, holding onto chairs or benches. A low ottoman helps him climb; if he can push it around, so much the better. He may end up on your cocktail table or on the window ledge—but just think what he's learning. By combining vision with locomotion, he is beginning to construct a three-dimensional world. Looking at the furnishings from all sides and positions, he sees many facets of them which were never apparent to him before. It is said that a famous four-star athlete once tried to imitate a baby's every move. He lasted for four hours, and then he collapsed!

In the midst of all this motor activity there is a fascinating new cognitive development. Slowly and gradually but nevertheless clearly, we watch the emergence of intentional, goal-directed behavior. According to Piaget, the ability to coordinate means

and end marks the beginning of intelligent activity. When the child can use familiar schemas to attain new goals, he has arrived at a landmark in sensory-motor development. We see this demonstrated in the manner in which he tries out and discards various ways of exploring a new situation. At the beginning, he will use a familiar schema perfected during Stage 3 to achieve a new result that he has never attempted before. In this case he is using it not to reproduce an effect already experienced accidentally, but as a way of exploring a novel situation. For example, in the following observation Piaget describes Jacqueline applying her grasping schema to an unfamiliar object, a cigarette case. When she can't reach it, she tries her shaking schema, a behavior she has habitually used for swinging her dolls.

At 0;8(20) Jacqueline tries to grasp a cigarette case which I present to her. I then slide it between the crossed strings which attach her dolls to the hood. She tries to reach it directly. Not succeeding, she immediately looks for the strings which are not in her hands and of which she only saw the part in which the cigarette case is entangled. She looks in front of her, grasps the strings, pulls and shakes them, etc. The cigarette case then falls and she grasps it.

In the previous stage the baby would use one particular schema every time he perceived one particular object (pulling a string to shake a hanging doll, or striking to produce noise from a rattle). Now he begins to combine and coordinate these schemas, applying them in new and unfamiliar situations. We are watching the growth of these behavior patterns from mechanical repetitive forms to what Piaget calls *mobile schemas*—flexible units of behavior adaptable to many more situations.

In addition, we are seeing here for the first time truly goal-oriented, intentional behavior. Previously it was difficult to separate the object of the activity (seeing the dolls swing) from the activity itself (shaking the dolls). Now we observe the goal as a separate end in itself which the baby may achieve by trying alternative actions or even by combining actions. Thus Jacqueline tried first to grasp the cigarette case; when that didn't work she tried the familiar shaking schema. In so doing she formed a new and more complex schema of shaking-in-order-to-grasp, which eventually enabled her to get hold of the cigarette case. We sometimes see different parts of the body used this way. If a child can't reach something with his hands he may push it toward himself with his feet until it is near enough for him to grasp. This is common among children whose movement is restricted by a walker or a feeding table.

Another form of means-end behavior is that in which the child uses the parent's hand in order to achieve a desired result, or to accomplish something he cannot do himself.

> At 0;8(13) Jacqueline watches her mother who is swinging the flounce on the bassinet. As soon as she stops, Jacqueline pushes her hand to make her continue. Then she herself grasps the flounce and

imitates the movement. That evening Jacqueline swings a hanging doll in the same way, with great delicacy.

At 0;10(30) Jacqueline grasps my hand, places it against a swinging doll which she was not able to set going herself, and exerts pressure on my index finger to make me do the necessary (same reaction three times in succession).

The parent's hand, here used as a means to an end, is sometimes seen as an obstacle to be pushed aside. Previously when Piaget hid objects behind his hand, his children no longer searched for them. Then Laurent tried to reach a matchbox by sliding around Piaget's hand, apparently trying "to take no notice of it."

Finally, at 0;7(13) Laurent reacts quite differently almost from the beginning of the experiment. I present a box of matches above my hand, but behind it, so that he cannot reach it without setting the obstacle aside. But Laurent, after trying to take no notice of it, suddenly tries to hit my hand as though to remove or lower it; I let him do it to me, and he grasps the box. I recommence to bar his passage, but using as a screen a sufficiently supple cushion to keep the impress of the child's gestures. Laurent tries to reach the box, and, bothered by the obstacle, he at once strikes it, definitely lowering it until the way is clear.

In this instance, the sight of the box calls forth the schema of grasping it. But when Piaget's hand intervenes, the goal of getting the box is postponed while Laurent looks around for a means to get rid of the obstacle. He turns to his familiar striking schema, which he uses first on his father's hand and then on the cushion that bars his way. Once he has got rid of these obstructions, Laurent proceeds to his goal of grasping the matchbox. This appears to be a clear example of intentional behavior carried through to a successful conclusion. It shows not only that the child is capable of purposive, goal-directed actions, but that he is abandoning "magical" repetitive schemas in favor of realistic behavior adapted to specific situations. This ability to maintain awareness of a goal while trying out different ways of reaching it is, Piaget says, an indication of intelligent action.

It is one thing, however, to proceed toward a visible goal as in Laurent's case, and quite another to locate one which is not visible. We have shown how, for the child in the previous stage, out of sight was out of mind. Now we observe a new phase in the development of the child's understanding of the permanence of objects. This is in his search for hidden objects.

Piaget's attention was first drawn to this phenomenon by the behavior of a cousin of his children. During a visit by the little boy, Piaget noticed a curious thing. Gérard, who was thirteen months old, was playing with a ball in the living room. When it rolled under an armchair, Gérard scrambled after it on all fours and managed, with some difficulty, to get it out from underneath. The next time he dropped the ball it rolled under a sofa at the other end of the room. Gérard saw it pass under the fringe of the sofa and tried to recover it, but it was too far underneath and the fringe got in his way. So Gérard got up, crossed the room to the armchair where the ball had first disappeared, and crawled under it, carefully looking for his ball!

This observation gave rise to a whole series of experiments in which Piaget hid objects first in one place (A) and then in another (B), all in full view of the child. Piaget was astonished to find that all three of his children at nine or ten months of age, even though they had watched him hide an object at B, went directly to A to find it.

At 0;10(9) Lucienne is seated on a sofa and plays with a plush duck. I put it on her lap and place a small red cushion on top of the duck (this is position A); Lucienne immediately raises the cushion and takes hold of the duck. I then place the duck next to her on the sofa in [position] B, and cover it with another cushion, a yellow one. Lucienne has watched all my moves, but as soon as the duck is hidden she returns to the little red cushion A on her lap, raises it and searches. An expression of disappointment; she turns it over in every direction and gives up.

After a few weeks of exposure to these experiments, Piaget found that his children began to go first to position B, but if the object had been hidden too well or displaced to a third position C, they would return to the original position A and search there "as though nothing had happened in the meantime!" Not until some time later were the children able to go directly to the one spot where they had seen the object hidden, ignoring all other positions.

Piaget thought about all this for a long time, and finally came to the conclusion that the children's behavior was not due to lack of observing where an object had disappeared, nor yet to inability to locate objects in space. The problem was that the object did not as yet have an independent existence. It existed in each position as an integral part of the action connected with placing or finding it at that position. Thus for Gérard there was a ball-under-the-sofa, but there was also a ball-under-the-armchair. When he could not find a ball-under-the-sofa he went back to the armchair where his activity had previously been successful, and looked for the ball where he had found it before. He still was not fully aware that the two images were one and the same ball. They were seen as the objects of two different actions, instead of existing as two different positions of one objective and permanent reality.

Piaget supported his thinking with several fascinating observations of his children after they were old enough to talk. At fifteen months, Lucienne was in the garden with her mother when she saw Piaget coming home. She smiled at him, but when her mother said, "Where is Papa?" Lucienne pointed up at the window of Piaget's office, where she was accustomed to seeing him. Again, when she was a year older, Lucienne was in the garden *with* her father. Hearing noise in his office upstairs, she said, "That is Papa up there."

From observations such as these, Piaget developed the hypothesis that "the object is still not the same to the child as it is to us: a substantial body, individualized and displaced in space without depending on the action context in which it is inserted." Lucienne recognized her papa, but in different aspects: Papa-at-his-window and Papa-in-the-garden were positions from which the independent image of "Papa" had not yet been totally abstracted. For a long time in the child's thinking, objects (including people) exist in a context, related to certain actions; they remain as extensions of the effort and the actions by which the child finds them again. The child in this fourth stage is looking for hidden objects in the context in which they were first seen or acted upon. It is only gradually that he becomes able to take account of successive displacements in space, and to look for the object where it was last seen. As he ignores ball-under-A or ball-under-B and moves directly to position C, he is showing a dawning awareness that the ball is a total, objective reality which exists apart from the positions in which it may be temporarily located. Again, Piaget is showing us how knowledge is constructed from action, and how the notion of object permanence develops out of many and varied experiences of objects in action.

It is no accident that the understanding of spatial positions shows such advances toward the end of the first year. As the child struggles to his feet and learns to maneuver about the house, he is much more exposed to the reality of objects in space. He must learn to get his body up and down without falling, and to deal with the world from many different positions. Stairs hold a special fascination at this stage, with their changing views from above and below. Babies will spend long periods of time practicing on them. If you can put your gate across the third or fourth step instead of the top or bottom one, you can give your baby room to practice without the danger of falling down a whole flight of stairs.

Christopher had already learned to climb the three steps to his back door when he came to spend an afternoon at my house. He started immediately for my stairs, which fortunately are thickly carpeted, and with me right behind him, he began the long climb up. The front door at the foot of the stairs was open, and Chris could see the trees and the sunlit walk outside. He would go up two or three steps, turn around, and look down at the distances below. Then a few more steps and another look back, all accompanied by excited chortling and gurgling. Finally he reached the top step and looked down with joyous triumph, surveying how far he had climbed. To come down, he soon learned to flatten himself out on his belly and slither down with amazing speed.

All spatial relationships are interesting to the baby now. He is learning on a sensory-motor basis the meaning of *up* and *down*, *inside* and *outside*. He studies the spaces within objects and the way they fit together; nested mixing bowls or measuring cups are fascinating to take apart. He explores the cavities in his body and in the bodies of those around him. Not only his parents, but other caregivers may be subjected to poking and jabbing little fingers exploring their eyes, ears, and teeth. Grandparents with gold fillings may find their mouths a source of great curiosity. I once came upon Jeffrey sitting on the floor side by side with his cousin of the same age. Jeff had one forefinger stuck in the other boy's ear as straight and firm as if he were sharpening a pencil!

Another motor development that has a part in all this exploration is the fine motor coordination of the fingers, the pincer movements that permit delicate picking up and dropping of bits of food, beads, small pebbles, leaves, and even worms. A baby at this stage will drop wooden beads into a can, pick buttons out of a jar, and tear your daily paper to shreds, all in the insatiable pursuit of knowledge about his world. He is fascinated with electric light switches, partly because they click and partly, I suspect, because of the magical power they give him to plunge the world into darkness. He loves things that open and shut. You may find him in your kitchen slamming the cupboard doors over and over again as he studies the mechanisms of hinges and latches.

Feeding time may become a special problem during this stage because with his new manual dexterity, the baby wants to hold his own spoon and feed himself. Try to guide his hand toward his mouth by putting your hand under his elbow. If that doesn't

work, let him hold his own spoon while you get your licks in with another. Or give him finger foods that don't require spooning. Your baby will probably drop bits and pieces over the edge of his high chair, particularly if he has an appreciative pet who gobbles them up. But try to accept the mess with good humor—it's an important part of his learning. If it becomes a struggle of wills between you (and certainly you've realized by now that your baby has a will of his own), the feeding situation can develop into a battleground which may have unpleasant associations for years to come. So when he tries to feed his vegetables to the cat, just smile and tell yourself: "In a hundred years, what will it matter?"

Imitation begins to appear more clearly toward the end of the first year. Babies will now imitate actions which they can see performed, such as hitting two blocks together, even though their first attempts are only an approximation of the adult's model. They may also imitate movements which they cannot watch themselves perform, such as blinking or yawning, as long as the movements are familiar to them. At eleven months Piaget had Jacqueline rubbing her eyes in imitation of him, or putting her finger in her ear. These were movements which she had already made herself, even though she could not see herself. Some babies have been taught to make faces, click their tongues, or give a Bronx cheer. Such games are lots of fun for both participants, though sometimes they may be carried too far. I remember teaching Christopher, at ten months, to imitate a little dry cough, after which we both laughed uproariously. A few days later I got a call requesting that I "decondition" Christopher. He had been coughing and giggling continually ever since, and his parents had had enough.

Vocal imitation may be increasingly evident during this stage. The baby's babbling begins to assume the rhythms and intonations of the speech he hears around him. He may produce a stream of gibberish that sounds almost like language, even though it makes no sense. If you listen carefully, you may be astounded to hear a familiar word here and there. I know one mother who angrily hung up the telephone and heard her little daughter mimicking the tone of her last remarks perfectly, ending with a clear and unmistakable "Damn!"

Imitation is important because it indicates the beginning of memory and representation. The baby has an image, a model which he remembers and represents by his own actions. As we pointed out earlier, the ability to deal with representations characterizes the period of intellectual development following the sensory-motor period. Vocal imitation is particularly necessary in the development of language, in which sounds become symbols for objects and actions. That is why it is so important that you talk to your baby, because every time you use a word like "spoon" in

conjunction with the object, he is learning the connection between objects and their names. Long before he can talk, your baby shows that he understands simple statements and questions and commands such as "Time for lunch," "Where is Daddy?" or "No, no!" He probably recognizes his name, and those of his family and pets. This is known as *receptive* language (see Chapter 9). During this stage, if you have conversed and played with your baby all along, he can imitate you in pointing to his body parts when you ask: "Where's your mouth? . . . Show me your eyes. . . . Where's your belly button?" The baby will enjoy your pleasure when he performs correctly, and he will begin to get the idea that certain sounds go regularly with certain familiar things. This is the beginning of language, and like so much of learning, it is rooted in a loving relationship.

The baby's loving relationships now increasingly include fathers, siblings, and close family members. What little research there is on the role of the father in infant development suggests that fathers who are available and take an active part in playing with their babies are as important as mothers very early in their children's lives. In fact, a study of twenty infants by Michael Lamb indicated that at seven or eight months babies of either sex seemed to prefer their fathers to their mothers for physical kinds of play. They tended to go to either parent for soothing and comfort in distress, although there were differences in the way these babies related to fathers and to mothers. As more fathers assume the role of primary caregiver, it will be interesting to see whether infants will cling to them and identify with them as they do now with their mothers.

In any case, as the baby grows increasingly active, it is understandable that either a girl or a boy would turn to the father to be tossed high in the air, carried on his shoulders, or engaged in joyous roughhousing. But if the play becomes a little too rough or the baby gets too far away from his mother, he may want to crawl back to her for comfort and reassurance. After all, he is becoming increasingly aware of his growing mobility. When he first rolls or crawls away from her, he looks back at her, triumphant in his achievement. But then he becomes aware of the distance he is putting between them. This contributes to his growing sense of himself as an individual. It also scares him a little when he realizes that he can separate himself from his mother, the source of comfort and protection. He may cry for her, holding out his arms, or he may paddle back to her for a hug or a reassuring pat. Mahler uses the term *emotional refueling* to refer to this

frequent return of the baby to his mother for reassurance of her presence and her love. Like a car running out of fuel, he comes back to the source of his emotional energy to "gas up" for his next trip.

This is a time when the mother must be sensitively attuned to the needs of her rapidly growing child. Some mothers feel so fulfilled in the close symbiotic relationship of earlier months that they cannot bear to let go of the baby. They keep holding and hugging him when he is squirming to escape and explore the world for himself. This creates frustration and eventually resentment. Other mothers are constantly fearful that the child will hurt himself, and keep running to rescue and protect him. This communicates fear and inhibits initiative. Still other mothers lose interest in their children when they are no longer "doll babies" and tend to ignore them. This is the greatest hurt of all.

I remember one insensitive mother talking at length on the phone while her little girl sat at her feet, holding onto her legs and gazing up at her with enormous, beseeching eyes. The mother could have scooped her baby up onto her lap, or smiled at her and patted her head without ever interrupting her conversation. Instead, she was fostering a fear of rejection in the child, who was wilting like a flower at her feet. Rather than sparking her intellectual curiosity, the youngster's natural energy was being drained by her attempts to draw from her mother the reassurance that she was loved.

Most parents, however, are happy to see their babies grow and develop, and they constantly communicate this to the child through encouraging words and smiles. If a mother tends to be overprotective, the father may approve of independence (or vice versa), so that parents supplement and balance each other's relationships with the child. The father's emotional support becomes especially important to the child of either sex from about eight months until around three years of age. This encompasses the whole period in the course of which the youngster is separating from his parents physically and psychologically, and becoming his own person.

During this time the child is most vulnerable to the fear of being parted from his parents that all children experience to a greater or lesser degree. The term *separation anxiety* is loosely used to cover many variations of this fear, from the whimpering, clinging behavior of the baby when his mother puts on her coat to the terrified screaming of the child whose parents are forced to leave him in a hospital. Its genesis is understandable when we remember that, for the baby, unseen objects do not exist. He cannot yet foresee that the parent who leaves him will return, and therefore his fear of abandonment is very real and very terrifying. This deep-seated fear is something that most of us live with to some degree all our lives. It is the basis of many anxious, uncomfortable feelings ranging from homesickness to the fear of death. In children, separation anxiety is most clearly seen between the ages of about eight months to three years. It may seem to be outgrown, and then reappear in even more exaggerated form. However, by the time a child learns to walk and talk and be somewhat self-sufficient, he usually isn't quite so dependent on his parents or quite so terrified when they go away for a little while.

But the eight- or ten-month-old baby is aware only of the immediate present. If his parents leave him in a strange situation, he may behave as though he had been completely abandoned. The fears that are often at their height at this age make it a bad time for the mother to start working, or for parents to take a vacation together of more than a day or two. Of course, every baby is different, and these generalizations may not apply to your child, especially if you leave him in his own home with a familiar person. However, separation anxiety is a frequent enough phenomenon so that you should be aware of it and recognize the symptoms. Don't be surprised or reproving if your cheerful, ebul-

lient baby clings to you or cries when you leave him. It indicates
that he knows the difference between you and other people and
doesn't want to be parted from you. It doesn't mean he is being
a "baby"; on the contrary, it shows that he is growing up. This
is a continuing process about which we will have more to say in
later stages.

At about this time in your baby's life, you may notice that he
is becoming attached to some special object such as a blanket or
a soft toy. The "Peanuts" cartoons have immortalized Linus's
"security blanket" as the prototype of all such cuddly, comforting
objects. With some babies it is a particular diaper or a stuffed
animal. Its importance usually emerges when you discover the
baby won't go to sleep without it. If it is a blanket, he may wind
it around himself and suck his thumb while stroking the binding
with his fingers. Holding and being held by the blanket re-
produces for the baby the warmth and closeness of being held in
his mother's arms, while his thumb replaces her nipple. Particularly if he is being weaned, as is frequent around six to eight
months, he may find substitute comfort in snuggling up to a soft,
pliable object which reminds him of his mother's body. It

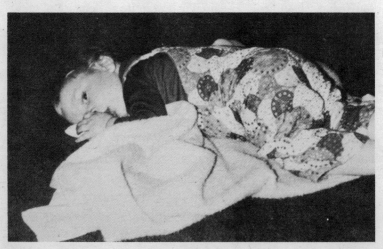

becomes a cherished possession which forms a link b
and his mother when she puts him to bed and leaves
Soon he begins to drag it around with him, and may
out of the house without it. Particularly in strange or stressful
situations, he will cling to this object, even when it gets so filthy
that it is a source of embarrassment to his parents. I never saw
this behavior more clearly demonstrated than by Jeffrey, who very
early became attached to a blue blanket with a silky binding like
his mother's robe. Whenever he felt tired, hurt, or insecure, he
would lie down on top of his blanket, bury his face in it, and suck
his thumb. After a few minutes of quiet retreat from the world,
he would get up and dart into the thick of things again, as active
and as cheerful as ever.

Usually children outgrow these precious possessions by the
time they are four, but they can be of great comfort in traumatic
situations such as a hospitalization. So try to bear with these
beloved objects, threadbare and decrepit though they may be.
Remember that to your baby, this is a symbol of his close relationship with you. When he no longer feels the need of it, he himself
will leave it behind.

TOYS AND GAMES

Beginning with this stage, the kinds of toys and play opportunities that your child has are very important to his cognitive development and to the strong motivation that early learning arouses
in him. The learning that has taken place up to now occurs in
almost all children without any special attention. But when the
baby reaches the level of intentional exploration, he needs parents
who will set the stage for him by establishing safe limits and
supplying interesting materials to be discovered and manipulated.
That is why it is important for you to know what achievements

your baby is working toward at any age level, and how to provide the materials that will challenge his interest and give him appropriate experiences. Dr. Burton White, whose research I have described, feels that "the educational developments that take place in the year or so that begins when a child is about eight months old are *the most important and most in need of attention of any that occur in human life*" (italics his).

The baby at this age is interested in anything that opens and shuts or fits into something else. Nesting toys or colorful plastic doughnuts on a spindle are appropriate; so are the popular sorting boxes with blocks that fit into round, square, or triangular holes. However, you can supply homemade toys which are just as satisfying. An ingenious mother I know cut round, square, and triangular openings in the plastic tops of three empty coffee cans so her son could fit the geometric forms of his wooden beads into the correct can. Cooking pots and mixing bowls that nest inside each other are great fun to take apart. Steel mixing bowls make wonderful sounds when whacked with a serving spoon. The covers of cooking pots can be spun like tops on a hard kitchen floor until they clatter to a loud finale. Jeffrey loved to open the steel drawer

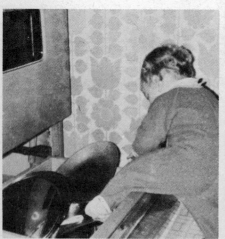

under my oven, dump out all the pot covers, and then climb into it himself. There he would sit and screech with pleasure while Chris and I made the covers spin noisily.

Putting things in order by size or length is the beginning of what Piaget calls *seriation,* a cognitive operation that underlies the concept of number. Children in school must learn to count, measure, and understand the relative places of first, second, and third. Their logical understanding of serial relationships grows out of years of concrete experiences of putting things in order, thus constructing the notion that sizes progress from small to big or from short to tall. That is why stacking toys graded in size are important for the baby.

Classification, the ability to group objects on some common basis, is another logical operation which has its roots in sensory-motor experience. In my house a favorite toy with small visitors is a wicker picnic basket containing four plastic place settings. Each one has a plate, a cup, and eating utensils in one of four different colors. At first children simply take them out; later they learn to put them back in the basket. After some random combinations they begin to fit the plates and cups into stacks. Finally they match up the sets by color. This is the beginning of classification on the sensory-motor level. Children may classify many things in many ways. Their bases for classification may not seem logical to adults, but it is only through a series of "wrong" solutions that children finally arrive at "right" answers. The important thing is that they be given the freedom to figure out the answers for themselves.

One good toy you should buy now is large blocks. The little square alphabet blocks are meaningless to your baby; he needs big rectangles he can pile up. Rather than buying hardwood blocks quite yet, I suggest you get the hollow ones manufactured from heavy corrugated cardboard. They are popular in many nursery schools because they are inexpensive and amazingly durable. Most important, they won't hurt your baby if they tumble down on him.

To give practice to agile little fingers, you can provide a plastic spool rack from your sewing basket, with empty spools to fit on the spindles. Or you might install hooks and latches on the back of a door for your child to practice on. An electrically knowledgeable parent could make a low-voltage battery-operated "busy box" like that designed by a friend of mine. It is equipped with plugs and switches, to allow children to experiment safely. There is a pull chain that turns on a tiny red light, and a switch that turns on a green one. A push button rings an electric doorbell, and the plugs are sturdy and safe. This is the perfect toy for all prying fingers, and is as popular with girls as with boys.

"Peekaboo" is still a favorite game; babies now begin to be active participants instead of just delighted observers. When they start to get around rapidly, "Hide and Seek" becomes a preferred variation in the search for the unseen person. It takes a long time before the baby learns the reciprocal nature of the game. Even

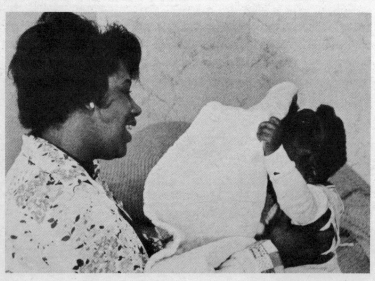

when he realizes it is his turn to hide, he may simply creep into a corner and put his hands over his eyes. Because he can't see you, he assumes that you can't see him; such is the egocentrism of babies and ostriches.

When I first began to hide from Christopher, I noticed that he always looked for me in the places where I had hidden before. If he was used to finding me in back of the couch, it never occurred to him to look behind the door. I began to give a little call so he would learn to follow the sound of my voice. I was surprised at how long it took before he could judge distances and directions from my auditory clues. We adults do this so instantaneously that we don't realize what an extended learning process we once had to go through.

Your child may now be ready for more advanced games in his search for the hidden object. If he has learned to find a toy that he watched you hide under one cover, try using two covers such as a diaper and a towel. Be sure they are unpatterned and plain enough so you know the baby is reaching for the toy and not for the covering. Also be sure they are both equally bunched up in the middle. With your baby watching, hide the toy under one cover a few times and let him find it. Then hide it under the other cover and see whether your baby (1) searches first under the original cover, (2) gives up when he doesn't find it there, or (3) goes directly to the second cover and removes it.

If he does the last, it means he has an image of the object as separate from the action of placing it under the first cover, and that this image is strong enough to last through the process of displacement he has witnessed.

When your baby is consistently successful at this game, try it with three covers—say, a diaper, a towel, and a cushion. From here on you can make up variations to fit your child's level of development. You can change the order of A, B, and C; or you can stack all three covers so that the toy is buried underneath. You will find more ideas as you read about Piaget's games in the next chapter.

Always be careful, however, that you correlate these hiding games with the developing stages of your baby's intellectual growth. As you hide a toy in different places, you are encouraging him to construct a stable image of the particular toy, regardless of where it is hidden. In the last step mentioned, the toy is hidden under a number of superimposed covers. The child may pull off one or two and give up by the time he reaches the third. Either he has lost interest (in which case STOP) or he does not have a strong enough image of the toy in his mind to last through the removing of so many covers. Next time, show him where it is, and let him watch again while you cover up the toy; or better yet, let *him* hide it. Remember, children learn by doing, not by being shown. Most important of all, don't make a lesson out of it. You're playing a game for fun, not pushing your child to be a genius. Here again we face the delicate problem of "match"—you must match your games to the child's level of interest and maturity, and not to your adult expectations for him. Remember that knowledge of the hidden object comes about very slowly; your child will not fully master it until he is well into his second year.

CHAPTER 5

Beginning to Experiment

Stage Five—12 to 18 Months

Your baby's first birthday is a major landmark both for him and for you. He is scarcely recognizable as the tiny infant of a year ago, whose chief interest was in searching for the nipple. Now he has several teeth and eats solid foods. He probably says a few words such as "Mama" and "Dada." But the biggest change of all is that somewhere around his first birthday he begins to walk.

You have watched him preparing for this for a long time: learning to roll over, push up on all fours, crawl, sit alone, and finally to pull himself up and cruise around the room, holding onto the furniture. There may be several weeks during which he walks about holding onto your fingers with both hands. Then comes the great day when he takes his first staggering steps alone! Parents should not push him too early or urge him too much if he seems afraid. "To stand unsupported, to take that first step is a brave and lonely thing to do." But when his muscles are mature and he is ready, he will take off, his face alive with excitement and the joy of mastery. A little fearful of finding himself launched into outer space, he may carry a toy or some object in one hand, as if for needed support.

For most children, the next few months are a very happy time in their development. The new toddler is highly elated as he sets forth, upright and alone, on a new series of adventures. Now begins his "love affair with the world"! Everything looks fresh and inviting from his new perspective. He takes off as if he were Superman, oblivious to danger. You will have to watch him carefully for a while, but try not to intervene unless he's really in trouble. The only way he can learn to manage his own locomotion is to experiment by himself. What are a few falls or bumps to a joyous toddler who's off to conquer the world? As long as you are around to swoop him up in your arms and comfort him, he will keep trying until he succeeds.

The first problem that faces him as he stands alone is how to get down again. Is there anything more comical than the struggles of a beginning toddler to get his fat little rear end safely back onto

the floor? He has to learn to bend, to squat, to stoop, or to let himself down holding onto the furniture. Sometimes you catch him, halfway down, peering at the world between his legs as if intrigued by this new perspective. Many, many times he practices each of these segments of behavior. Gradually he gets them all together into the new, enlarged schema of getting-up-and-walk-ing-and-sitting-down-again. As his locomotion becomes smoothly coordinated and manageable, the toddler turns to all the tantaliz-ing new discoveries that await him.

Now comes the age of experimentation. The child wants to know more and more about objects—how they react and how they are related to each other in space. Previously he explored things by taking them apart; now he tries to get them back together. He begins to stack blocks instead of knocking them over. He fits containers inside each other, or drops small objects into a tin cup, listening to the difference in sound between a metal ring and a wooden bead. He will spend hours taking an old percolator apart and trying to put it together again. In front of the mirror, he will study his reflection very carefully, experiment-ing first with one movement, then with another, as he tries to sort out what is himself and what is his image.

The child of this stage has been exploring for a long time, but

now he seems to experiment much more scientifically. He no longer applies new schemas in a repetitive way, but varies them as if to find out how the results will differ. It is as though he is realizing that objects act independently of him, and he is studying their possibilities. Piaget calls this *directed groping*. He describes his little son Laurent, who was breaking bits off a piece of bread and dropping them systematically at different places on the floor around him. Like a young Galileo, the boy was watching with absorbed interest to see where the bread would land. If he dropped it in front of him, the bread landed in front; if from the left side, the bread landed on the left side. This may seem unnecessarily messy experimentation to parents with years of experience with the law of gravity, but for the child it can be a fascinating discovery.

One lovely autumn afternoon Christopher, just past his first birthday, was left with me for an hour. I took him outside to see the Japanese rock garden which had been newly laid out along the slopes of a steep bank behind our house. It was in the form of a dry stream bed, with many smooth white rocks and pebbles of different sizes forming a cascade that curved down the hillside, around miniature pines and Japanese maples, to the edge of the lawn. Christopher regarded it with interest; his first move was to put one of the rocks in his mouth. When I took it away and threw it back in the stream bed, the rock landed with an interesting "clack." Thereupon Christopher picked up another rock, and another, dropping them to hear the sound. He discovered that some rocks were too heavy for him to pick up, and would grasp my hand to get me to help him. Others he could handle well, and would throw them as best he could in different directions, watching to see where they landed. Then he tried throwing some of the autumn leaves that had fallen on the rocks, and found that they behaved in an entirely different way. We spent a fascinating hour in the garden, experimenting with the gravities and trajectories of falling objects.

In this kind of behavior we see the essential difference between the young infant's behavior schemas and those of the year-old child. The infant's schemas are repetitive, centered around himself and his efforts to master his body movements. The older he gets, the more his interest moves outward to his environment. By the fourth stage he is examining objects, sounds, and textures in the world around him in order to explore their possibilities, and combining schemas in new ways to achieve his objectives. In this fifth stage he becomes increasingly interested in the external results of his acts, which he varies in different ways in order to see what novelties he can produce. He is groping toward the discovery of new means, resulting in the development of new behavior schemas which can then be coordinated with the old ones. Thus the child's repertoire of behaviors grows ever more complex and more adaptable.

Piaget uses the term *new means* to refer to new ways of carrying out goal-oriented activities. There is a change in the child's means-end behavior which is characteristic of this stage. Whereas previously he had used his parent's arm and hand as an extension of his own, now he begins to use sticks, strings, or other objects to achieve his ends. One of these new means was noticed by Piaget when he watched his children learning to obtain toys they could not otherwise reach by pulling toward themselves the cushions or bedcovers on which the toys rested. Jacqueline, as early as nine months, got hold of a celluloid duck by pulling toward herself the coverlet which supported it. Piaget felt that this was probably an accidental discovery, since it was not repeated until two months later. By around a year, however, Jacqueline was regularly pulling a shawl or cushions toward herself in order to retrieve her toys. Laurent made the discovery at ten and a half months old, after some previous experience.

> I place my watch on a big red cushion . . . and place the cushion directly in front of the child. Laurent tries to reach the watch directly

and not succeeding, he grabs the cushion, which he draws toward him as before. But then, instead of letting go of the support at once, as he has hitherto done, in order to try again to grasp the objective, he recommences with obvious interest to move the cushion while look-ing at the watch. Everything takes place as though he noticed for the first time the relationship for its own sake and studied it as such. He easily succeeds in grasping the watch.

Piaget also gives detailed descriptions of how his children dis-covered the uses of strings or chains to pull objects toward them. He tied a string to Jacqueline's hairbrush, or used his watch chain to make it possible for her to reach his watch. For Laurent he laid out winding trails of string to lead to his favorite red shoehorn, and watched to see how long it would take him to make a connec-tion between the two. This is not an immediate discovery, as I learned by tying a long yellow ribbon to Christopher's favorite rattle when he was about ten months old. He pulled the ribbon, and the rattle moved toward him. I was waiting breathlessly for him to retrieve the rattle, but Christopher was more interested in the ribbon. After chewing on it a bit, he noticed the rattle moving, so he promptly crawled over and got it, ignoring the yellow ribbon. Toddlers often do not understand what to do with pull toys, particularly if they get them too soon. They do better at first with push toys, such as a musical roller with a long handle. It takes a while for them to make the connection between the string and the toy attached to it, and to pull it after them.

During this stage the toddler also learns to use a stick as a new means quite separate from any toy. A stick can be made to push or pull or move, a discovery that grows out of the striking schema of Stage 2. While a string is an extension of an object, a stick is an independent instrument; it takes a good deal of practice with striking and pushing before the child notices that he can bring an object nearer to himself in this way. A pinwheel was an object of great interest for Jeffrey, at first for its visual effects, but later as a means for striking brass bells or a Japanese wind chime hanging on the porch well above his head. Eventually he even used the pinwheel as a fly swatter, whacking at insects on the porch screens. In the same way, Jacqueline's use of a stick as an instrument was the culmination of many hitting and prodding experiences:

> Finally, at 1;3(12) she discovers the possibility of making objects slide on the floor by means of the stick and so drawing them to her; in order to catch a doll lying on the ground out of reach, she begins by striking it with the stick, then, noticing its slight displacement, she pushes it until she is able to attain it with her right hand.

All of these experiences of pushing, pulling, and moving help the child to recognize that objects have their own properties apart from his actions on them. In the course of his experimentation he begins to notice the sequence of positions through which objects may roll or fall or bounce. Instead of following these displacements with his whole body, he can now watch them with just his eyes; and eventually he can anticipate where the action of rolling or falling will end up. He can then go directly to the last position in which an object is seen and find it there. This behavior indicates that the child now recognizes the independent existence of the object apart from the places in which it has been hidden, as Piaget notes in the following observation.

> At 1;0(20) Jacqueline watches me hide my watch under cushion A on her left, then under cushion B on her right; in the latter case she immediately searches in the right place. If I bury the object deep she searches for a long time, then gives up, but she does not return to A.
> At 1;0(26), same experiment. At the first attempt Jacqueline searches and finds in A where I first put the watch. When I hide it in B Jacqueline does not succeed in finding it there, being unable to raise the cushion altogether. Then she turns around, unnerved, and

touches different things including cushion A, but she does not try to turn it over; she *knows* that the watch is no longer under it.

This certainty of Jacqueline's is characteristic of the fifth stage of development, according to Piaget. The child is now able to follow *visible* changes of position, but is still mystified when faced with *invisible* displacements. As the following observation shows, Jacqueline can follow visually but not logically. When Piaget places a box with a potato in it under a rug, and brings out only the empty box, Jacqueline cannot reason that the box went under the rug full and came out empty, and that therefore the potato must be under the rug.

> At 1;6(8) Jacqueline is sitting on a green rug and playing with a potato which interests her very much (it is a new object for her). She says "po-terre"* and amuses herself putting it into an empty box and taking it out again. For several days she has been enthusiastic about this game.
>
> I then take the potato and put it in the box while Jacqueline watches. Then I place the box under the rug and turn it upside down, thus leaving the object hidden by the rug without letting the child see my maneuver, and I bring out the empty box. I say to Jacqueline, who has not stopped looking at the rug and who has realized that I was doing something under it: "Give papa the potato." She searches for the object in the box, looks at me, again looks at the box minutely, looks at the rug, etc., but it does not occur to her to raise the rug in order to find the potato underneath.

Jacqueline at this stage still could not follow invisible displacements. In the succeeding days Piaget continued to play with her, showing her his ring in his open left hand before surreptitiously slipping it into his right. Then he would hold out both his closed fists to her and let her open them each time until she learned to look first into one, then into the other. After that, Piaget placed

---

Pomme de terre is French for "potato."

the ring in one hand, put his hand into a beret, and withdrew it still closed. Jacqueline opened the closed hand and, finding no ring, looked all around, but not inside the beret. So she reverted to her earlier pattern and insisted on looking inside Piaget's other hand, which had no part in this experiment. Like Gérard who went back to the armchair (see p. 67), Jacqueline was guided by the memory of actions which had succeeded in the past rather than by awareness of present relationships. As Piaget observed, she was operating on the basis of "practical learning and not a deduction of the relations themselves." On the higher plane of invisible relationships she was repeating all the steps in learning through which she had previously passed on the plane of visible relationships.

The problem of children of this stage, according to Piaget, is that they are not yet capable of mentally imagining or representing to themselves what is happening to objects that they cannot see. It is not just that the child cannot remember the sequence of displacements as they occur, but that he has not yet completely constructed a concept of the object independent of its position in space. This is an extension of what we saw happening in Stage 4 on the visible level. There the child learned to recognize a ball, for example, abstracted from its various positions under-the-armchair or under-the-sofa. Now he must construct a mental image or representation of that ball so that he can follow its various movements in his mind even when there is no visible object. Jacqueline, for example, could not yet do this with the potato. Although she looked around for it, she could not represent to herself mentally what must have happened to it, and therefore did not know where to look for it. Not until later was she capable of the mental imagery that characterizes the next period of intellectual development.

It is interesting that the mental image of the beloved parent seems to be forming in the child's mind earlier than his representations of physical objects. Usually the mother is by far the most stimulating object in the child's life long before he becomes emotionally attached to her. Think of the many sensory ways in which she can be experienced, even at the level of inborn reflexes. She can be sucked, and the milk gives her breasts a distinctive smell and taste. Even if the infant is bottle-fed, he recognizes the mother's familiar odor, and the touch and feel of her body. We have already noted how early the baby responds to his mother's face and the sound of her voice. She is an ever-changing phenomenon, sometimes near, sometimes far, sometimes heard but not seen. She dresses in different colors and responds to the baby's needs in a kaleidoscope of varying moods and expressions. No wonder he spends so much time watching and listening to her!

Because he is so close to her, so much a part of her, the baby comes only slowly to the realization that his mother is a separate individual. As we have seen, he begins by responding with a special smile to her voice and presence. By the time he is about six months old, he recognizes her and other familiar people, and is wary of strangers. By eight or nine months he will cry if he is separated from his mother too long or too suddenly. When he begins to crawl away from her, he checks back frequently to be sure she is near. This may involve just looking around at her, or calling her until he hears her answering voice. But all of this suggests that the child has in his mind the image of a familiar and beloved person who may be out of sight but is not out of mind for very long.

As the toddler learns to walk, he moves into the exhilarated period we are now seeing, in which the world is his oyster. But even during this time, his spirits may be dampened if his mother leaves him. He may look repeatedly toward her empty chair as if picturing her there, or stand by the door through which he saw her leaving. It is as if he misses her and summons up a mental image of her to comfort him.

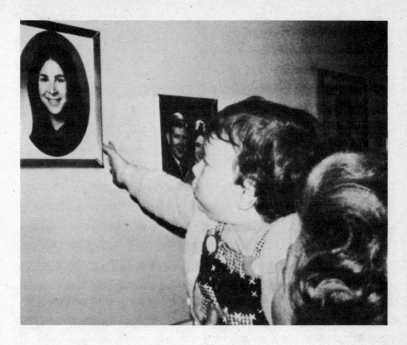

When Christopher was just past one, he spent a weekend with his grandfather and me. He was on my bed and I was changing his diaper when he suddenly began pointing and babbling to me at a great rate. At first I didn't know what he wanted. Then I realized that he was pointing to a smiling photograph of his mother which hung on the bedroom wall along with several others. He had never noticed it before, but now he recognized her and wanted to touch and talk to the picture. He was crying a little, but it seemed to comfort him to see her face, perhaps because it reinforced his own inner image during her absence.

Mahler has described this behavior in the toddlers at her center. A child may be so busy playing, she says, that at first he doesn't even notice his mother's absence. But when he looks around and finds her gone, it is as if some of the joy had gone out of his activity. He becomes what Mahler calls "low-keyed": a little depressed, a little withdrawn. He may cry over small hurts or bumps he never would have noticed before. When his mother returns, it's as if the sun had come out from behind the clouds, and the world is bright again.

Most of the time, however, the beginning toddler is practicing his new skills with such concentration that he doesn't even look around to see where his mother is. He simply takes off, seeming to assume that she is right behind him, ready to swoop down and ward off all dangers. As the toddler grows more sure of himself, he sometimes seems to resent his mother's protection. He may shout "No!" at her, push her away, or kick and scream when she picks him up. This is the beginning of the well-known negativism of the young child. He is struggling to establish his own autonomy, to become an individual separate from his all-encompassing mother, and it's not easy!

According to Dr. Ernst Abelin, who has studied parent-child relationships at Mahler's research center, the role of the father assumes added importance at this time. The familiar mother is taken for granted, but the father is the newer and more exciting parent. He is different from the mother who provides a safe "home base" for occasional refueling. When the father returns from work in the evening, he is often "greeted with greater joy and excitement than the mother has evoked all day." The father is more active in his physical play and will run and throw and gallop with the exuberant toddler (who has probably exhausted his mother already!). It is understandable that he seems a glamorous and exciting alternative to the well-known (and perhaps well-worn) mother.

So it is not surprising if, as Abelin's observations indicate, the father should become the preferred parent, and perhaps ally, of the child who is trying to become independent of his mother. By imitating this big, masculine model, he can avoid slipping back into being "Mama's baby" again. He carefully watches his father shave and perform other bathroom rituals. He wants to use

Daddy's tools to hammer, saw, and fix things. Jeffrey loves to lug an old attaché case around the house in imitation of his father. Both boys and girls are very interested in their fathers, and sometimes respond to other men as well in an affectionate and trusting manner. There are, of course, enormous variations in the way individual fathers interact with their children; sometimes little girls are treated quite differently from boys. Nor are fathers always around to be masculine models for their children. However, when they are available, fathers are an important influence in the lives of their babies, and this influence increases as the children grow older and can use them as models of both physical enjoyment and intellectual pursuits.

TOYS AND GAMES

Toys that aid in locomotion are very popular with children of this age. They like small, low kiddie cars, though they may turn them over and merely spin the wheels at first. Little wagons can be pulled, and doll carriages can be pushed. Toddlers love to imitate Daddy with a miniature plastic lawn mower or a little wheelbarrow. I have already mentioned the round music box on wheels that is pushed with a stick; another push toy like it is a "corn popper" that pops up plastic balls.

Probably the most useful present I ever got for Christopher was a two-step kitchen stool. He still drags it all over the house to help him reach things in cupboards and closets, and it is certainly safer than pulling out drawers and using them as steps. It enables him to stand at the kitchen counter and cut out cookies, switch on the electric blender, and generally participate in what's going on. It's also useful for getting up to the sink for water play, and for looking out the window.

Toys that develop large muscle coordination such as balls and pounding pegboards are always good for toddlers. Small muscles come into play also, with the development of pincer finger movements. Your baby will enjoy picking up pegs or wooden beads chosen carefully to be too large to swallow. Anything that can be taken apart or put together, such as nested pots or an old percolator, is a source of endless pleasure. On my buffet I have a pair of teakwood candlesticks that fit together in sections. Jeffrey's first activity when he comes to visit is to climb up on a chair, remove the candles, and systematically take the candlesticks apart. You undoubtedly have equally intriguing objects in your home which your child will discover. I often think these are more interesting to the child when he's *not* invited to play with them. If he can

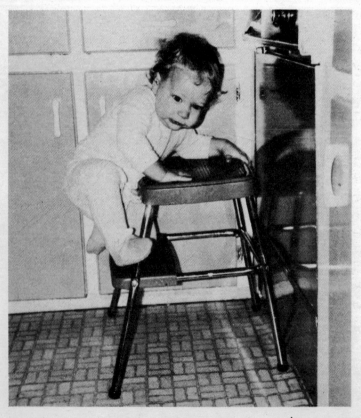

master the things he sees his parents use, instead of playing with childish toys, doesn't that make him more of a big person like them?

In view of Christopher's response to his mother's photograph which I described earlier, I began to use the family photo album as a picture book for him. He loved to look at photos of his parents, grandparents, cousins, and pets, and most especially of himself! It wasn't long before he was naming all of us as he pointed to our pictures. If you don't want to endanger your family album, give your toddler one of those plastic cubes with six photographs of his family to enjoy.

Storybooks can become a bit more sophisticated now, for your child understands much more language and is probably beginning to talk. If he watches *Sesame Street* on TV (don't expect that he will be interested for more than a few minutes at a time) he probably knows some letters and numbers. Alphabet books and counting games like "Ten Little Indians" now begin to have some meaning. Children's records are often too "talky" for him, so play your own favorites. Good music, like good art, knows no age level, and your child will absorb it through his pores without even being aware that he's learning it by listening.

Favorite games are still hiding games such as those I have already described. You can also invent obstacle games. Build a low wall of hollow blocks between the child and his favorite toy, and let him knock it down to reach his goal. A sheet of plexiglass or a clear lucite chopping board makes an interesting obstacle. The child sees the toy but can't reach it, and has to figure out an alternative approach. As he gets older, you can make the task harder. Hide a pull toy, but leave the string visible. Put a toy out of reach, but give the child a stick or a plastic rake with which he can retrieve it. When he goes looking for unseen toys by himself, with a clear and intentional plan of search, you will know that he has achieved object permanence.

CHAPTER 6

On the Threshold of Thought

Stage Six—18 to 24 months

By the middle of his second year your toddler is getting around very efficiently. He can walk, he can run, he can climb, he can get into almost anything. He clambers out of his crib at night and trots back into the living room, turning on all his charm to persuade you to let him stay up with you. Or he invades your bed, perhaps frightened by a bad dream but more likely just wanting the reassurance of his parents' warm bodies. He may not have much language, but his gestures and intonations make his wishes very clear. He imitates his parents in ways that show how much he wants to be like them, using tools or caring for dolls. I remember watching Christopher trying on his father's shoes and looking appalled at how much he would have to grow to fill them!

But even that small act showed a certain amount of foresight; it involved mental rather than mere physical experimentation. This is characteristic of the child who is moving into the final stage of the sensory-motor period. According to Piaget, he appears to be experimenting less and less on the external, physical level and more and more on the internal, mental level. There seems to

be a new awareness of relationships, without the necessity for as much physical trial and error. It is as if the child could foresee which manipulations will succeed and which will fail. Piaget describes how Jacqueline came into the house with a blade of grass in each hand. Wanting to go outdoors again, she put the grass on the floor so that her hands were free to open the door. But as she was pulling the door toward her she realized that the grass was lying in its path and would be caught under the door. She stopped to pick up the grass and move it to a safe place before she went back to finish opening the door.

This is only a tiny incident, yet it shows the little girl's ability to represent mentally to herself what would happen, based on numerous past experiences. Jacqueline realized that she could not open the door when her hands were full—undoubtedly the result of many previous sensory-motor acts. She also foresaw what would happen to her precious blades of grass if they were caught in the path of the door. So she *mentally* invented a solution, which would provide a safe place for her treasures.

What the child is working toward in this stage is the ability to invent new means through internal, mental coordinations of schemas, rather than through visible sensory-motor experimentations. It is a long, slow process and does not take place all at once. Many sensory-motor behaviors from previous stages will continue to persist, but the peak achievement of this final stage is the appearance of *representation*. Representation, according to Piaget, can be a copy of the absent reality such as an imitative sound or a memory image, or it can be a symbol only distantly related to the object it represents. In make-believe play (see Chapter 8), stuffed animals may represent babies and sticks may be used as guns, even though there is little resemblance to what the symbols portray. The words used in language are arbitrary sound symbols which are unrelated to what they represent and must be learned. We will discuss the development of language in Chapter 9; for the present, however, let us observe the slow emergence of symbolic representation at the close of the sensory-motor period.

Piaget's most famous example is that of Lucienne and the matchbox. At sixteen months, Lucienne was busy getting Piaget's watch chain out of an empty matchbox. When the box was uncovered, Lucienne had no trouble in turning it over and dumping out the chain: she had already had plenty of experience in emptying other receptacles such as her pail. Then Piaget slid the cover onto the matchbox part way, leaving a wide opening for Lucienne to poke in her index finger and grasp the chain. This she did successfully, although Piaget did not let her see how he slid the cover onto the box.

Next, Piaget closed the matchbox almost entirely, so that only a little slit remained open at one end. Lucienne tried to put her index finger in but could not reach the chain. There was a long pause while she surveyed the box; then Lucienne did a very curious thing. She looked attentively at the slit, and then she began to open and shut her mouth—only slightly at first, but then wider and wider. Lucienne was imitating with her mouth what she wanted to do with the matchbox. Without actually touching the box, she was acting out with her mouth what she must do to it in order to get it open. After thus symbolically representing her actions to herself in advance, Lucienne without hesitation put her finger in the slit. No longer did she try to reach the chain; she simply slid open the box far enough so that she could pull it out without difficulty. Lucienne was on the verge of thought!

The capacity to represent actions mentally instead of acting them out physically results, of course, in a dramatic saving of time. The child is no longer groping for solutions; he gives the impression of suddenly understanding the problem. I remember sitting on the floor with Christopher, trying to figure out how to hook up the cars on a little wooden train set just received from

Sweden. Obviously Christopher at just past two had considerably more linking schemas available to him than did his grandmother. He took the cars out of my hands, turned one around, and hooked it up perfectly. *"I did it!"* he said triumphantly. He had grasped the relationship of the different ends of the cars far faster than I had, and his success made him feel competent to tackle harder problems.

This ability to capitalize quickly on past experience, using a repertoire of mobile and flexible schemas, is one important factor in the final achievement of object permanence. The other is the ability to make deductions about the movements of an object which is not visible. We saw in the preceding stage that Jacqueline could not deduce that her potato was under the green rug because she did not see Piaget put it there; her concept of object permanence was still limited to visible objects. When she has fully achieved the idea of objects as independent and permanent, existing whether she is aware of them or not, her behavior becomes quite different, as the following observation shows.

> At 1;7(23) Jacqueline reveals herself to be equally capable of conceiving of the object present under a series of superimposed or encasing screens.
>
> Before her eyes I put a pencil in a strainer (which I turn over on the floor). I place a beret on the strainer and a coverlet on the beret; Jacqueline raises the coverlet at once, then the beret, then the strainer, and takes possession of the pencil.
>
> Then I put the pencil in a closed matchbox which I cover with the beret and the coverlet. Jacqueline raises both screens, then opens the box.
>
> I put the pencil back in the box, put a piece of paper around it, wrap this in a handkerchief, then cover the whole thing with the beret and the coverlet. Jacqueline removes these last two screens, then unfolds the handkerchief. She does not find the box right away, but continues looking for it, evidently convinced of its presence; she then

perceives the paper, recognizes it immediately, unfolds it, opens the box and grasps the pencil.

Here Jacqueline obviously assumes the existence of the pencil, no matter how complicated its hiding place. It has become an independent object for her, subject to its own laws of displacement quite apart from her actions upon it. Furthermore, she has a mental image of the pencil, a representation of it which guides her in her search for it. In other words she is *thinking* about the pencil and *remembering* where it had previously been hidden. These are cognitive activities taking place internally rather than externally. Their emergence is a major milestone in the child's intellectual development.

Another evidence of mental representation is the child's growing ability to imitate. We have watched him imitating sounds and gestures that were immediately present; now we begin to see what Piaget calls *deferred imitation*. This refers to imitation that takes place after the actual object or event is no longer visible. The child is now able to construct mental images that are remembered later on. A dramatic example of this is given in the following observation.

At 1;4(3) Jacqueline had a visit from a little boy of 1;6, whom she used to see from time to time, and who, in the course of the afternoon, got into a terrible temper. He screamed as he tried to get out of a play-pen and pushed it backwards, stamping his feet. Jacqueline stood watching him in amazement, never having witnessed such a scene before. The next day, she herself screamed in her play-pen and tried to move it, stamping her foot lightly several times in succession. The imitation of the whole scene was most striking. Had it been immediate, it would naturally not have involved representation, but coming as it did after an interval of more than twelve hours, it must have involved some representative or pre-representative element:

At 1;4(17), after a visit from the same boy, she again gave a clear imitation of him, but in another position. She was standing up, and

drew herself up with her head and shoulders thrown back, and laughed loudly (like the model).

Imitation here is no longer dependent on external events; it has become internalized. It may appear in many forms, conscious and unconscious. We often observe the feminine wiles of little girls or the bold swagger of little boys as they unconsciously imitate their parents or older peers. Dr. Berry Brazelton describes "whole chunks of behavior" which may be picked up by one child watching another. Certainly many civilizing activities such as table manners, putting away toys, brushing teeth, and "taking turns" are acquired largely through imitating and identifying with admired models.

A recent study by Dr. Ina Uzgiris suggests that an important outgrowth of the imitative process is the child's differentiation of his own self from those whom he imitates. She studied twelve babies regularly for two years, presenting them with sounds and gestures to be imitated. They ranged from simple, familiar noises and acts to unfamiliar, complex movements and new words. In general she found, as did Piaget, that by the end of the first year the babies were actively trying to accommodate to new experiences by reproducing her behavior as closely as they could. Their approximations became more accurate during the second year, and even unfamiliar sounds and gestures were imitated fairly directly. But Uzgiris noted that the babies' reactions changed as they began to differentiate between their own and the experimenter's acts. For example, when Uzgiris rubbed her hand with a cotton ball, the younger babies also rubbed her hand. Only later did they rub their own hands, showing their realization that the act was supposed to be performed on themselves. Uzgiris suggests that imitative acting contributes to the development of a sense

of self, as well as to the development of mental imagery leading to conceptual thought.

So we see that the child by about two has completed the Copernican revolution which Piaget described. He realizes that he has an identity and is a part of a much larger world, instead of being the center and sole inhabitant of his egocentric universe. We have watched this change come about through the daily round of sensory-motor experiences which the child assimilates and reconstructs for himself. First there were only the simple, instinctive reflexes of the newborn. Gradually these were combined with each other by chance, then repeated and smoothed out until they became well-established schemas. Then these schemas were coordinated with each other in a variety of ways, at first accidentally, and then intentionally, in order to prolong interesting sights and sounds. The infant "watches and finds more to watch; follows and finds more to follow; turns towards sounds and sees as well as hears; comes to look at what he grasps and to guide grasping through looking; manipulates and produces effects which then prompt him to repeat his actions till he can produce them at will." By the end of the first year the baby is searching for objects not seen, pushing aside obstacles, showing evidence of anticipation and intentional behavior. At each stage new behavior patterns emerge and are superimposed on previous behaviors so that the structures of intelligence grow like an ever-widening spiral with each loop showing more complex, better coordinated, and better integrated schemas of adaptive behavior. Looking backward, we can see how far the child has come.

But now a curious contradiction arises between the child's growing competence and his emotional insecurity. The more independent he appears, the more dependent he seems to become! Intellectually, he is making the big leap from sensory-motor activity to mental activity, or thought. Physically, he grows more capable every day. Yet, toward the middle of his second year, this

busy, lively, "runabout" child is likely to show a resurging dependence on his mother. He seems to realize that he is a very small
child in a very big world and needs his mother more than ever.
At the same time, feeling his physical strength and struggling to
establish his own identity, he fights his mother and resists adult
controls. He is caught between a new intellectual awareness of his
dependence on her and a growing emotional need to become
independent of her. Therein lies his conflict.

How does this conflict show itself in the child's behavior? For
one thing, he may follow his mother about the house, wanting her
to talk to him, to play with him, to admire whatever he is doing.
On the other hand, he may run away from her, carried away by
his new-found mobility, and then be frightened if she does not
dart after him and bring him back to safety. This is an exhausting

stage for mothers, because older toddlers are often strong and willful and can put up a real battle. I have seen a little girl kicking and screaming as her mother tried to remove her from a fountain in the middle of a public plaza. (I would have been tempted to let her fall in, since it was a warm day and a shallow fountain. Certainly she would have learned her lesson a lot more effectively!) Another mother was terrified when her little daughter escaped from her grasp and started up the "down" escalator by herself. This is the age when the greatest number of accidents and poisonings occur. Children are physically very mobile, but they are not yet aware of the imminent dangers surrounding them. They don't understand language enough to grasp their mothers' warnings. All they hear is "No!"—which they soon learn to hurl back at their parents.

But gradually there comes to every child an awareness of the fact that he is very small and vulnerable, and it is his mother who protects him. As the realization of his ability to run away from her dawns on him, he sees her increasingly as a separate person from himself. Gone is the old magic of babyhood, when his mother seemed ever present and all powerful, shielding him from harm. He is confronted with the fact that she is not a part of him, that she has needs and interests of her own, as well as relationships with people other than himself. There is the private life she shares with Daddy, from which he feels himself excluded. If she should be pregnant at about this time, he may find her less and less responsive to him, unable to chase him about and roughhouse with him. Or if she should decide to go to work, the child has to cope with being separated from her all day long, which may be more than he can understand or accept.

Up to now the child has experienced fear of strange people and situations, and fear of being physically separated from his mother. Now, in his second year, he finds himself faced with a new fear —the fear of losing his mother's love. His reaction can range from occasional jealous competition with other family members to overwhelming feelings of abandonment if she goes off and leaves him too long. Depending on the severity of this fear, the child clings to his mother and woos her in every possible way. No longer does he seem almost oblivious to her absence, as in the early, exhilarating days of learning to walk. Now he may grow increasingly restless and distractible when she is away. He may hurt himself very easily and cry, demanding her attention. He may regress to previous babyish ways, or show disturbed sleep patterns. All these are danger signals that he is unduly upset about his relationship with his mother, which makes him anxious and insecure.

Not every child, of course, has this hard a time separating from his mother. Fathers assume increased importance at this age and can help a great deal, especially if the mother has a job or a new baby. There is a special fascination about fathers: their size, strength, and masculinity intrigue children, and in most homes they cannot be taken quite so much for granted as mothers can. Sometimes they are stricter, sometimes more easygoing, than

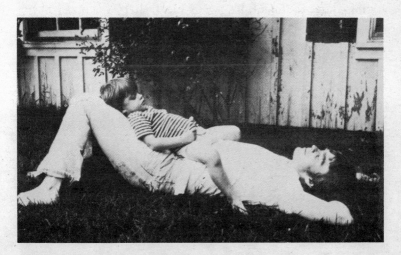

mothers; in either case they help the toddler learn to adjust to different personalities. Coming up against the father helps the child of either sex to define his or her identity in new and different terms. The little boy models himself on the male image, learning to talk like his father, imitate his activities, and use his tools. Little girls, responding to their fathers, learn to be feminine and charming, sometimes clearly imitating their mother's mannerisms. The wise father will be careful not to react in a seductive way to such behavior, beguiling though it may be.

Growing up is made much easier by the gradual development of language that occurs around this time. The child learns to ask for what he wants; he finds he can get his mother's attention just by calling her. When he uses expressions like "Hi!" and "Bye-bye," he is delighted to find that others understand and respond to him. He now enjoys playing near other children ("parallel play") and finds pleasure in appearing to be involved in social relationships, even if he is too young to really take part in other children's activities.

When the child must be separated from his mother, it helps a great deal if he is with a familiar person and/or in familiar surroundings, preferably his own home. If that is not possible, give him a chance to get acquainted with the new premises in advance: go with him to visit the babysitter's home, or take him on a tour of the hospital. Let him bring along some of his most precious possessions—his familiar blanket, some favorite toys, perhaps a picture of you. Many hospitals now permit parents to stay overnight with the child, which makes his time there much less terrifying.

Dr. John Bowlby, a noted English psychiatrist, has made a comprehensive study of children who are separated from their parents for prolonged periods. He finds that the first reaction is one of protest—kicking, screaming, and struggling to go after the departing parent. Then comes a period of despair, listless crying and signs of intense longing. One little girl refused to take her coat off for three days because "Mummy will be coming." Finally, in prolonged cases, there is an emotional detachment in which the child seems to deny any recognition or affection for the mother. It is as if he is saying: "You abandoned me; now I have given you up for lost."

These stages are of course modified by the circumstances of the separation (a loving grandmother versus a strange hospital, for example) and by the age and personality of the individual child. But babies and toddlers who are parted from their parents often show variations of these behaviors. If left for just a little while, they may cling desperately to the returned mother, but sometimes they will ignore her or refuse to go to her. It may take several days of alternating anger and affection before things are back to normal. When Chris was eighteen months old he was left with us for a five-day vacation. He seemed fine; this time he didn't even peer through the back door as he used to. But the night his parents came back, Chris shrank against me and screamed when his mother held out her arms to him. It was quite a while before she could take him home. He sat in my lap and seemed almost to be flirting with her—leaning toward her, and then turning away and ignoring her. Then followed a couple of days during which he was perfectly miserable to her before their usual affectionate relationship was restored.

Christopher's emotional ambivalence is characteristic of this stage of development: intensified love and longing for the mother is contrasted with rebellion, anger, and the fight to establish an independent identity. Children approaching the age of two grow increasingly stubborn and resistant; it sometimes seems they are out to exasperate their parents in every possible way. If you are in a hurry, your toddler will dawdle endlessly. If you want to sleep late, he will be up at dawn. If you are tired, he is bursting with energy. If you are listening for the weather report, he will imitate a fire siren. If you deny him something, he may have a temper tantrum, lying on the floor and screaming, or holding his breath until he turns blue.

Sometimes your toddler may even attack you, kicking, scratching, and biting. This is hard for even a loving mother to endure, and the impulse to strike back is very strong. But that only adds fuel to the fire, and puts you on the child's level of behavior. Try picking him up in a big bear hug and holding him so tightly that he can't hit you, while you talk him down. That doesn't mean reasoning with him—how can you reason with an angry, preverbal child? It means saying things like, "Lucy is very angry with Mommy. But Mommy isn't angry with Lucy. Mommy loves Lucy, and Mommy is going to give her a big hug, and then we'll have some nice supper"—or a warm bath, a quiet story, or whatever is appropriate to the occasion.

This kind of behavior, almost universal in pre-twos, often builds to a crescendo during the following year. The child has achieved physical independence; now he is struggling to achieve psychological independence as well (a preview of adolescent rebellion). Your toddler sets his jaw, plants his small feet firmly on the ground, and does exactly the opposite of what you tell him to do, just to prove that he is his own boss. I remember once having a phone conversation with my daughter. In the middle of something I was saying, she cried out, "Chris, don't do that . . . Chris, I said NO!" Over the phone, clear as a bell, I heard a defiant little voice answering, *"I* say ESS!"

What is a mother to do in a case like this? Well, first of all, don't despair. Millions of other parents (including your own) have been faced with similar behavior and lived to laugh at it. You may even be tempted to laugh yourself, but don't do it in front of the toddler. He may get the idea that he's cute, and give a repeat performance. Sometimes, as in the case of a tantrum, it helps to walk out of the room. What good is a performance without an audience?

Try to think about the reasons for this behavior. Is your child overly tired or hungry? Then feed him, or put him down for a nap. Have you been making too many demands on him? Ease up on table manners and postpone toilet training for a while. Is he upset because you're busy with a new baby or a job and don't have much time for him? Tell him you understand, and try to give him a special cozy private time of his own every day. Have you been unhappy, or worried about a sick parent or financial problems? Your child is very quick to sense your moods and react to them. You might tell him in very simple terms, "Mommy and Daddy are upset because Grandpa's very sick. But we're not upset with you, and we'll all be happy again when Grandpa gets well."

If you recognize your child's negativism as a part of his growing up, you might begin to give him carefully limited choices, so he won't feel he has to put up such a fight for independence. You could give him a choice of two outfits to wear, or two foods to have for lunch. You could say, "Do you want to go to the supermarket with me or stay home and play with Daddy?" You could even let him win an argument sometimes—not because he whined or cried, but because he convinced you. For example:

Child: I wanna ice cream.

Mother: No, it's too near suppertime.

Child: I wanna ice cream for *after* supper.

Mother: Okay, we'll buy it and put it in the freezer, and you can have it for dessert.

Here is a contest of wills in which there are no losers. Such a solution is not always possible, but the more you can treat your child pleasantly (even when he is unpleasant) and with respect for his budding individuality, the easier his growing up will be. Furthermore, he will be a better parent when his turn comes, if you can handle him with tolerance, understanding, and a warm sense of humor. Under the stress of anger, so many parents who really *want* to be good parents fall back on the ways their parents treated them. Time and again it has been shown that the parents of "battered babies" were themselves abused as children. Psychiatrists' couches are burdened with adults still fighting ancient battles with *their* parents. The only answer to this vicious cycle that I can see is for parents to understand themselves and their children. If you know what to expect from your child and why he is behaving in certain ways, you will be able to deal with him rationally and affectionately, even though he can be thoroughly infuriating at times.

Along with having a choice and other privileges of growing up, a child needs some of the responsibilities. Not enough is expected of children today: frequently, they don't share in family chores the way children did a generation or two ago. True, with modern machines there's less to do—and it's much easier and quicker to do it yourself—but children need to learn very early that they are expected to help. Even your toddler can put his soiled clothes in the hamper or smooth the covers while you are making the beds. The two-year-old can bring silverware to the dishwasher or put it away in a drawer. At three he can carry sorted laundry to the right bedroom, and help lug in the groceries (two tin cans in a paper bag aren't too heavy). Give him a pail of water and a brush and he will enthusiastically help you "paint" the house. As he wins your thanks and approval, he feels good about himself as a contributing member of the family.

TOYS AND GAMES

You can now begin to expect your child to help put away his playthings. If you provide open shelves for him, he can stow his toys away quite easily and also get at the ones he wants to play with, without calling for your assistance. A toy chest soon becomes unbelievably jumbled, and I'm always afraid of the lid slamming down on little fingers. If you find the shelves getting crowded with too many toys and books, put some of them away for a while, and bring them out on a rainy day. Most children have so many toys that they do not fully explore all the possibilities of each one. I also feel that many toys, in this age of plastics, are much too elaborate and detailed. They leave no room for the child's fantasy to fill in, no alternatives for his creative imagina-

tion. Simple handcarved cars and boats, beautifully shaped out of natural wood, are preferable to the brightly colored, intricate plastic creations which sell, alas, for much less. The same applies to dolls. A soft, simply dressed doll can be a baby or a bride or whatever the child's fantasy dictates. But many of the gorgeously dressed creatures in our toy stores today suggest a single role only and leave little to the child's creativity. Around two, many children are beginning to enjoy make-believe play, and their playthings should leave plenty of scope for the developing imagination.

Certain structured toys, however, do lend themselves to the child's needs at this age. A toy telephone not only encourages imaginary conversations but helps to develop language. Simple, sturdy, wooden puzzles help children to reconstruct a picture from the memory image in their minds, and thus reinforce the

image. Big, colored wooden beads to string provide a challenge to small fingers. Another small muscle skill that develops around this time is the ability to screw on bottle caps. Give your child a small plastic thermos or bottle with a cap that fits in his hand. Watch him, and see how difficult it is to master this coordination which seems so easy to you.

Pre-twos should spend a lot of time outdoors in active play. You are fortunate if you have a good playground nearby, where your toddler can watch other children and imitate their play on the slides and swings. Playground equipment is so expensive and so quickly outgrown that the use of a well-equipped public facility can save you money. Then you can hang up an old spare tire for a swing at home: it doesn't cost anything, and won't hurt much if it hits your youngster. A short, sturdy ladder nailed securely against a wall or a tree provides good climbing practice. One of the many kinds of foot-propelled vehicles is fine, but a tricycle is probably still hard to manage. If your child is having a difficult time controlling angry feelings, get him a punching bag to drain off some of his aggression, or an inflatable "Bozo the Clown" that will help him work out his rage without hurting anybody.

Sand play and water play are very valuable for learning about changing quantities and qualities. With shovels, pails, and measuring cups, children can empty and fill, pour and measure, for hours. Gradually they will learn about quantities and how they change in appearance as they are poured into different containers. This learning takes years, and is not fully acquired until about age six or seven. The little boy in the Introduction who wanted "a full glass of milk" was still judging by the appearance of the milk rather than its actual quantity.

Children learn about the qualities of sand and water, too: how sand changes character when it is mixed with water, and how wet sand can be shaped and manipulated, where as dry sand cannot. Sieves, funnels, and plastic bottles are fine for sand play, while gravy basters and egg beaters make wonderful water toys. So does a hose with an adjustable nozzle that changes the spray. But the best water toy I ever found for Christopher was a plastic water wheel. A funnel at the top emptied into a hopper, which in turn emptied onto the first of three water wheels. The wheels were interlocked in such a way that the water ran from each one onto the next, until all three wheels were spinning merrily. Christopher spent hours in the bathtub figuring out how the contraption worked. Then one day when he was about three, we went to visit an old colonial paper mill. The ancient water wheel was still creaking around, each paddle spilling the water onto the one underneath and making it turn. Christopher watched it for a long time in silence. Then he turned to me and said, "Grammy, I *know* how that works!"

This is true knowledge in Piaget's sense of the word: knowledge which is constructed from action upon objects. Christopher had experienced through his senses and through his own motor activity how such a water wheel worked. Now he could stand before an antique model and, simply by looking at it, grasp the principle upon which it was operating. Christopher was leaving babyhood behind.

CHAPTER 7

Symbols, Magic, and Monsters

The Third Year

By the time he starts his third year, your child is no longer a baby but very much a person. He is at home in his physical world; he knows where to find his toys and how to help dress and feed himself. He has a primitive understanding of space, time, and causality, which he has acquired through his experiences of the past two years. You have watched him learning to cope with three-dimensional space as he crawled or climbed or searched for a fallen toy. His ideas of time have developed around regularly occurring daily experiences: time for breakfast, bath, and nap; playtime, suppertime, time for Daddy and/or Mommy to come home. His understanding of cause and effect is similarly constructed out of many small experiments—kicking moves his mobile, flicking the switch brings light, pushing the ball makes it roll. Most important, he not only recognizes the independent existence of people and objects around him, but when they are absent he can represent them to himself through imitation, mental images, or make-believe play. And now he is acquiring the most abstract symbol system of all: he is learning to talk!

The two-year-old appears to have outgrown the "locked-in" egocentrism of infancy; certainly he is capable of dealing realistically with the physical world around him. Yet, despite his competence on the sensory-motor level, he has not come as far as it appears. Piaget's earliest research was on the thinking of the young child; he found that his thoughts and emotions, his understanding of the world around him, are still very much colored by his *psychological* egocentrism. Because *he* is alive and has feelings, he assumes that all else in the world is alive and conscious, too. The sun and the moon follow after him when he takes a walk; the wind is singing to him; the "naughty chair" hurts him when he trips over it. The child's belief in *animism*, in the consciousness of inanimate objects, is very like that of primitive tribes who believe a spirit dwells in every tree and spring, and perform ritual dances to persuade the gods to send rain. How similar to our familiar nursery rhyme in which the child issues the command:

> Rain, rain, go away,
> Come again another day.
> Little Johnny wants to play.

In this little rhyme we also sense the child's feeling of magic omnipotence, his belief that he can command the elements. He still has the feeling that the world was created for his pleasure and to do his bidding. The roots of this feeling, as we have seen, go far back into infancy, when the baby, lying in his crib, had only to whimper and a loving adult rushed to see what he needed. Food appeared when he was hungry; diapers were changed when he was wet; his wishes were anticipated almost before he was aware of them. Psychoanalysts point out the similarity of these experiences to ancient fairy tales of genies who appeared with loaded tables of delicacies or of fairy godmothers who granted the most outrageous wishes. This secret belief in one's own magical powers persists late into childhood, and vestiges of it are found in otherwise reasonable adults. Have you never carried an umbrella to make sure it wouldn't rain, or avoided cracks in the pavement so you wouldn't "break your mother's back"? Witness Jacqueline's magic omnipotence, described by Piaget in the following observation. (As his children grew older, Piaget referred to them by their first initials, except for Laurent, whom he called "T" in order to distinguish him from Lucienne.)

> When J. was 5;6(11) I overheard a conversation between her and L. in bed. L. was afraid of the dark and J. was reassuring her. L. then asked: "Where does the dark come from? *From water, because when it's daytime, the night goes into the lake.*" But at 5;6(22) I heard J. alone in the garden saying: *I'm making the daylight come up, I'm making it come up* (making a gesture of raising something from the ground). *Now I'm making it go away* (gesture of pushing something away) *and now the night's coming. I make the night come up when I go to the edge of the lake: the man* (walking outside the garden) *still has a bit on his coat. I'm making the light come up.*" After this she amused herself the rest of the day in *"making light"* with a stick (making the gesture of pulling it towards her and throwing it away).

This observation contains the seeds of another of Piaget's discoveries about children's thinking. Here Jacqueline was controlling the coming of day and night; by the end of the day she was "making light." One is reminded of the ancient biblical story of creation, in which God said, "Let there be light." Piaget found, through his perceptive questioning, that young children share these primitive anthropomorphic notions of creation. They believe that the sun and the moon are created by man, or by God who is very like a man. The sun's light comes from fire, or from a match lit by a man who then throws the flaming sun into the heavens. The moon is born quite small, "like us when we are little babies"; it grows "because we get bigger." Sometimes it is cut up by people who then "make it whole again." Clouds come from the smoke of chimneys, and mist from steaming saucepans. Jacqueline, at twenty months, looked at the smoke arising from Piaget's ever-present pipe and cried, "Mist daddy smoke!"

There is a basic contradiction between these two beliefs: one wonders how all things could be alive and conscious and still be created for and by man. But children are not yet concerned about logic; their thinking at this level is magical, contradictory, and egocentric, like that of primitive peoples. When Piaget first published the results of these studies back in the twenties, his readers were shocked and astounded. A well-known American psychologist, Dr. Wayne Dennis, was unconvinced. He tried out some of Piaget's questions on his little daughter, who was not quite three, and was amazed to discover that she, too, showed many of the characteristics of magical thinking described by Piaget. She even demonstrated for her father how she could make the rain come by dancing around the room! Dennis and many other psychologists did follow-up studies in various parts of the world and found that in general Piaget's ideas were correct. Most children *do* have the ideas I am describing in this chapter, although some have them so early that they have almost no language in which to express them. Here are some of the remarks made by Piaget's and other children which he recorded:

At 2;1   Moon running (following the child).

At 2;5   There aren't any boats on the lake; they're asleep.

At 2;5   (on a winter morning) Oh good! The sun's come to make the radiators warm.

At 2;6   The sun goes to bed because it's sad.

At 2;10   (looking at blowing leaves) Do they like dancing?

At 2;9   (looking at a hollow in a tree) Didn't it cry when the hole was made?

At 2;9   (watching a stone roll down a bank) Look at the stone. It's afraid of the grass.

Of course, times have changed since Piaget collected these responses. Because of the influence of TV, children may know a lot more about the world; certainly we would expect them to know more about the moon because men have landed there. Thus, imagine my delight when Christopher, at just past three, came out with an unsolicited story illustrating exactly what Piaget says about the child's anthropomorphic thinking. He and I were taking a walk one afternoon and looking at the sky, where the full moon showed white in the bright sunshine. Chris asked me, "Why does the moon shine?" In true Piagetian fashion I bounced the question back to him. "Why do *you* think it shines, Chris?" This is what he said:

> A fireman had a big, big ladder to go up to the moon. He put it way up in the sky, and the sky held it up. He went up the ladder to the moon with his flashlight. It was big, like a plumber's flashlight. He put it on the moon and let it stay there. It made the moon light up. When the moon was going down, he came quick to get his flashlight off the moon so it don't go down with the moon. Then he went down the ladder and put the flashlight in his firetruck and he bring it home where all the other firetruck is.

Notice how concrete is the child's thinking. The sky can hold the ladder up; the moon is lit with a plumber's flashlight which is bigger than average; the celestial fireman takes care not to lose his flashlight. If I had had my wits about me I should have asked Chris why the moon went down, for Piaget found that children consider that anything which moves, like clouds or a river, is alive and conscious. Try asking your child of two or so whether the wind or your automobile is alive and why. ("You know what it is to be alive? Your cat is alive, isn't it? Tell me something else that's alive. . . . Why? How do you know it's [not] alive?") You may get an answer such as I once did: "The wind is alive because it blows. When it doesn't blow, it's not dead, it's just asleep." Piaget found that not until the age of six or seven do children restrict conscious life to animals and people.

In fact, the age of about seven marks a turning point, Piaget found, in the child's intellectual development. He begins to think logically, to reason things out, and to be much more realistic in his observations of the world. The years before six or seven, from the end of the sensory-motor period to the time the child starts the first grade in school, are characterized to some degree by the illogical, intuitive, magical thinking we have been describing. Adults find it funny, puzzling, cute, or incomprehensible. We can understand it better if we realize that the child is slowly groping his way from a world of sensory-motor activity toward a world of thought. Mental activity must replace physical, and it does so by means of images and symbols. Instead of dealing with an actual object, the child forms a mental representation of it and deals with it symbolically as Lucienne did with the matchbox (see p. 103). Sometimes you see a child doing both simultaneously. I once watched a youngster struggling to cut paper with a pair of scissors, and noticed that her mouth was opening and closing as her fingers opened and closed the scissors. This was very similar to Lucienne's activities except that she wasn't touching the matchbox with her hands; the symbolic activity was taking place entirely in her head, and was only represented by her mouth.

Let us take a look at the kinds of symbols which the child can use. Probably the earliest are pictures; he has been recognizing pictures for some time, and now he begins to draw his own. He starts with scribbles which are fun on the sensory-motor level, and gradually approximates a lopsided circle. Christopher was almost three when he announced that one such scribble was his dog, and the other was Coco, his kitty. His mother pointed to the latter and said, "Is that your dog?" "No," said Christopher very firmly, "that Coco." Even mixing up the scribbles didn't dissuade him;

Christopher was quite clear in his mind about what it was he had been trying to represent.

Dreams are another form of symbolic representation that arise out of the physical experiences of the sensory-motor period. While infants sometimes smile or cry in their sleep as if they were dreaming, we have no evidence as yet that they dream, though there is some interesting research on dream-associated REM brainwaves of newborns. Piaget reported the first definite proof of dreams between 1;9 and 2, in children who talked in their sleep or described their dreams. One little girl woke up crying because another child who had taken all her toys the day before had reappeared in her dreams and upset her. At 2;8 another girl awoke with loud screams and explained, "It was all dark and I saw a horrid lady over there. That's why I screamed."

Obviously, to these children their dreams were very real. They could not distinguish between dreams and reality. In fact, Piaget found that children up to about five believed their dreams came from some external source and entered their bedrooms. One child would not even go back to bed in his room because it was "full of dreams." When Piaget asked children where the dreams came from, he was told, "From the night," "From the sky," or "They come when you shut your eyes."

Most children are six or seven before they realize that dreams originate in their heads and only *seem* to exist outside of themselves. In the meantime, your small child can be terrified by bad dreams. You can comfort him by holding him close and explaining that dreams are just pictures we see inside our heads when we are asleep. They may be scary, but they go away when we wake up, just as the TV picture vanishes when we flip the knob.

Some children develop all sorts of bedtime rituals in order to ward off these monsters of the night. They range from interminable delaying actions to arranging all the dolls or toy animals in a set order, as if to stand guard during the night. Other children touch every banister on the way upstairs, or insist on having the covers tucked in tightly all around them. Parents can help by giving extra love and reassurance at fearful, whiny times and lessening the pressures during the day. A night light in the child's room or a door open to the hall can help relieve anxiety. In time, children will learn to cope with the fears that life brings to all of us.

Other symbols we have already mentioned include those we learn by imitation, such as waving "bye-bye," wailing like a siren, or crossing oneself (a magical gesture to ward off evil). A very important step in the development of thought, according to Piaget, is the ability to engage in make-believe play. Here one is using a symbol to represent something which is not even present. Small boys using sticks for guns act out whole sequences of imaginary experiences in which most of the action is going on in their heads. The sticks are the symbols that mediate between overt sensory-motor acts and internal imaginary events, as we shall see in Chapter 8.

Yet another symbol system, and undoubtedly the most important one, is language. The symbols of language are words which have been agreed upon by a given society to represent certain meanings. There is no similarity at all between the word "dog" and the animal it signifies, so that children must painstakingly learn the names of many things during their early years. Probably the first of children's many questions is "Whaddat?" Knowing the right names opens up for the child a new source of power; he can demand things, command attention, and communicate his needs to others. Thus names become magical symbols of that which they represent. They exist as part of the thing or person named. Children cannot imagine that they could have been called by any other name; their names are a part of themselves. After he had learned to recognize his name, I gave Christopher a miniature license plate with CHRIS on it in big letters. One day when I saw it on his tricycle, I asked him what it said, "Me!" he announced proudly. In his thinking, "Chris" and "me" were identical and could not be separated. I was reminded of the faith of primitive peoples in voodoo magic and the power one acquires over another by learning his name. Even in fairy stories names are of great importance. No wonder Rumpelstiltskin was so careful to keep his a secret!

It takes some time before children realize that their names exist separately from themselves. When Piaget asked the nursery school children at the Maison des Petits where their names were, they said: "In the air," "Nowhere," or, "In all the houses which know it." One of my little neighbors told me that her name was in her pocket. I asked where it was when she undressed and went to bed at night, and she said it was under her bed. When I suggested that she might have been called by her sister's name instead of the one she was given, she was outraged. Yet her eight-year-old brother who was listening laughed at her and said, "A name is only a word your parents choose. The minister gives it to you [at baptism] but he could just as well give you another one."

This attachment to names as inseparable from the persons they represent gives us some idea of the rigid thinking of the very young child. He has difficulty dealing with more than one thing at a time because his ideas are so concrete. "Kitty" means only his particular cat. When he begins to learn that "kitty" also applies to the neighbor's cat, we see the first hazy, confused attempts at generalized thinking. It takes years before the child is able to abstract a concept of kitties-in-general, of which his particular cat is only one example. First he must have concrete sensory-motor experiences with many particular cats, which he assimilates to a gradually expanding schema of cats. (Here we use the term *schema* to include clusters of experience and information; eventually such a schema becomes a concept.) As the child's maturing intelligence is able to organize and catalog more and more information (i.e., baby cats are called kittens, Siamese cats have blue eyes, tigers at the zoo are a kind of cat), the growing schemas are integrated into concepts. The first fuzzy, overgeneralized concepts of the very young are what Piaget calls *preconcepts.* Later on these develop into the coherent and integrated concepts of the school-age child.

Piaget considers the preconcept as "halfway between the symbol and the concept proper." Its chief characteristic is that it is neither truly individual nor truly generalized, but fumbles about somewhere in between. The child hasn't had enough experience to understand the relation between representatives of a class and the class itself. He calls his father "Daddy" and then calls other men "Daddy" as well. This is a case of overgeneralizing, in which many representatives are lumped into a class which should apply to only one individual daddy. On the other hand, confronted by different representatives of the same class, the child may think that he is seeing repeated appearance of the same individual, like Papa-in-the-garden and Papa-in-his-office. In the following observation, Jacqueline distinguishes between bees and bumblebees, but doesn't differentiate between insects and animals. Moreover, one slug is just like the next slug to her, so she thinks it's the same one, rather than another representative of the same species.

J. at 2;6(3): *"That's not a bee, it's a bumblebee. Is it an animal?"* But also at about 2;6 she used the term *"the slug"* for the slugs we went to see every morning along a certain road. At 2;7(2) she cried: *"There it is!"* on seeing one, and when we saw another ten yards further on she said: *"There's the slug again."* I answered: "But isn't it another one?" J. then went back to see the first one. "Is it the same one? —*Yes.* —Another slug? —*Yes.* —Another or the same?" The question obviously had no meaning for J.

At 3;3(0) J. was playing with a red insect, which disappeared. A quarter of an hour later when we were out for a walk we tried to look at a lizard which darted away. Ten minutes afterwards we found another red insect. *"It's the red animal again. —Do you think so? — Where's the lizard then?"*

Not only does the preconceptual child lump together unrelated classifications as Jacqueline did with lizards and red insects, he is equally illogical about cause-and-effect relationships. Whatever happens together is causally related in the child's mind. Thunder makes the rain come, the road makes the bicycle go, and honking the horn will make the car run. "The cold is when the snow wants to fall," one child told Piaget. "It comes from the wind." Another said, "It is because we go to sleep that makes the night so dark." A little girl explained, "The moon doesn't fall down because it is too high up." My favorite bit of reasoning comes from Jacqueline, who said, "I haven't had my nap so it isn't afternoon." Christopher once wanted his mother to read him a story. She was busy just then, but when she went to him a few minutes later, she found him trying to put on her sunglasses. "Why do you want them?" she asked. "So I can read the story," said Christopher. "That's how Grammy reads—with her glasses!"

It is amusing, puzzling, and sometimes a real challenge to try to understand the reasoning of a very young child. It gives us a glimpse into the "non sequitur" logic of one who is struggling to understand a complex and varied world on the basis of limited experience. The egocentrism which permeates the child's thinking shows itself in many ways: in his magical thinking, in his illogical logic, in his inability to understand another point of view. Piaget was struck by this last when taking his young son Laurent for a drive around Geneva. Piaget's home is on the outskirts of the city, where a great, rugged mountain called the Salève dominates the landscape. Laurent had seen it countless times from his garden, and knew its name perfectly well. Yet on this drive he looked up and said, "What's the name of that mountain, Papa?"

Piaget was surprised until he stopped to think about it. Then he realized that Laurent was seeing the mountain from a different perspective, and therefore thought it was a different mountain.

Piaget then designed a series of experiments in which he placed on a table a miniature landscape with trees, houses, and a papier-mâché mountain. He put a doll in a chair on one side of the table and asked a child to sit facing the landscape on the opposite side. Then he gave the child photographs of the landscape taken from different points of view, and asked him to pick out the one that showed the landscape as he saw it. This the child could do easily. But when Piaget asked him to pick out the photograph that showed the landscape as the doll saw it, the child was unable to do so. He was limited to his own perspective and couldn't put himself mentally in the doll's place and imagine how the scene would look from there. The only way he could perform the experiment successfully was to change places with the doll and actually see the scene from the opposite side of the table.

This kind of egocentric thinking affects the emotions as well

as the judgment. Little children do not have the capacity to put themselves "in the other person's shoes" and understand how he feels about things, which is why it is so important for parents to understand the child's point of view. This egocentric attitude is the source of most children's fights when they begin to play together. In the third year, children are becoming social beings who need and enjoy playmates. They begin to seek out their peers and imitate them, picking up not only language but social skills. Learning to share and to take turns, however, is not an easy lesson for the very young who have no concept of how other people feel.

Watch a visiting child try to play with his host's favorite toy, and you will hear screams of "I wannit; it's *mine!*" A struggle may ensue in which somebody will get hurt, unless an alert adult is nearby to provide a quick substitute. If you ask the assailant why he hit little Carol, he will reply with complete justification (in his eyes), "She tried to take my toy!" If you say, "But you hurt her. You don't want to hurt Carol, do you?" you are wasting your breath. It takes a good deal of experience and maturity before a child begins to understand and empathize with the feelings of his peers. That is why children just learning to play together need careful supervision. You don't have to be obtrusive about it, however; children sometimes learn more if adults appear to be ignoring them. Chris was once playing with two little girls whom he knew very well, and he was being particularly obnoxious. One of them picked up a Frisbee and then looked cautiously in my direction. I turned away casually, but out of the corner of my eye I saw her give Christopher one good whack with the Frisbee. I had decided it wouldn't hurt him, and he might learn a lesson from it. The problem in supervising children of this age is to appear unconcerned while not missing a thing. In this way, they work out their own problems more effectively, and you're available to prevent actual bloodshed.

While two-year-olds are quite willing to inflict damage on each other, they are inordinately concerned about small scratches or bruises to themselves. So fearful are they of any bodily injury that this has been called "the year of the Band-Aid." The small child has only recently gained motor control of his body and developed a sense of himself as separate from his mother. In a large and sometimes threatening world, he finds himself extremely vulnerable. With every cut he sees his life's blood oozing away, and it is very reassuring to him to be plastered up by Mama and thus made whole again. This feeling of vulnerability leads to a gradual decrease in the child's sense of magic omnipotence. Realizing his own weakness, he invests more power in his parents, those all-powerful, all-knowing, all-giving ones from whom all good things come. "My Daddy is stronger than God," he will brag, or "My Daddy could kill a burglar." Which brings us to the subject of monsters.

For sometimes daddies get very angry at children, and a daddy who could kill a burglar might also kill someone else if he were angry enough! Spankings may raise just such fears in a child, even though they may sometimes be necessary. But too often the child does not understand the connection between his misdeed and the punishment that follows, particularly if there is a time lapse in between. He only understands that his loving father has suddenly turned into an angry monster, and this fills him with rage and terror. He may have nightmares in which he is chased by wicked ogres or fearful giants, and from which he wakes up screaming. These terrifying creatures may represent the wrath of his father or they may symbolize the child's own pent-up anger which he dares not express against so powerful an adversary. Sometimes children will scream, "I hate you, I wish you were dead!" But this is a very dangerous attack for the child to make against the source of all his well-being, and he is more likely to suppress such feelings out of fear. In that case the anger may come out symbolically in his dreams, and with it the guilt for ever having had such feelings.

The child's own emotions may turn on him to punish him in his sleep.

Children seem to have occasional bad dreams when they are less than a year old. But screaming nightmares, together with negativism and temper tantrums, are what make parents sigh over "the terrible twos." They should remember that the child is under a great deal of pressure during this period in his development. He is struggling desperately to control and direct his own life. He wants to feed himself, and may end up plastering food all over himself or pouring milk down his front. He doesn't want to lie still and have his diapers changed any more, and the battle to clean and dress him may set off a full-scale rebellion. (Better to change him standing up if necessary.) Yet for all his self-assertive ways, the two-year-old is still terribly dependent on his mother. He may be suffering from separation anxiety, discussed earlier, which shows itself in weepy, clinging behavior and unwillingness to go to bed for fear Mother won't be there if he wakes up. He may cry out frequently during the night or demand his worn security blanket as a substitute for her.

In this period of fears and body vulnerability, many children are afraid of being washed down the bathtub drain. If they keep asking where the water goes, or how it goes down, just explain that only water goes down the drain, never children. Youngsters are likely to be even more afraid of being flushed down the toilet. They see that whirlpool of rushing water which sucks everything down with it, and are terrified that they might fall in. Then there are all the weird noises that go on inside the tank. "What kind of monster lives in there?" some children wonder. To be perched atop that Niagara Falls on a wobbly seat high off the floor is very frightening to many children. They are likely to be more comfortable on a low potty seat, particularly if a parent keeps them company on the grownup toilet.

The mother who pushes her child toward toilet training when

he is not ready may be creating even more problems for herself. The young child may not really understand what it is that his mother wants him to do. If she can catch him at the right time, he may succeed in producing what she wants. But if she wants it so much, why does she promptly flush it down the toilet and make it disappear forever? And if he can't produce and makes her angry, will she then make him disappear too? For the two-year-old the situation is fraught with inexpressible fears and fantasies. After all, that warm brown thing is a product of his own body, which he labored and brought forth. He may be quite interested in examining it, and be upset when it is flushed out of sight. He may also be so affected by mother's expressions of disgust that he then becomes very concerned about cleanliness and is afraid to get his clothes dirty for a long time afterward.

Sometimes children resist toilet training as a way of rebelling against mothers and expressing new-found independence. It is another way of saying "No!" to Mommy which she really can't do much about. She can keep the child strapped to the seat for an hour, but he can get back at her by defecating in his pants the minute he gets off the toilet. Obviously, this kind of struggle between a harassed mother and a willful child can lead to all sorts of problems. The best thing to do is not to try to train your youngster until you are sure of success. If he is battling through a siege of negativism, wait until that phase is over and he's more calm and cheerful. At strategic times, ask him whether he wants to go—and don't leave him on the seat for more than a few minutes. Some children are easy to catch: their faces flush; they strain and make what Christopher calls "poopy noises." If you can catch your child at such a time, and express pride and pleasure in his performing like a "big boy" or girl, he will probably want to please you again. I had a sister who was so positively conditioned that when she wanted to go to the toilet, she always said, "I want to go good girl." A more modern youngster of my acquaintance rises from the pot with upraised fist and shouts, "Right on!"

Bladder control comes later and more gradually, but it is usually achieved somewhere around the age of three. There may be accidents at night for a while, but most children like to be clean and dry, and are upset when they wet the bed. So don't add to your child's distress, and if it happens too often, particularly after he has been dry for a while, try to find out what circumstances may be putting undue stress on him.

All of this training takes time—but then growing up is a slow process. Somewhere around the middle to the end of the third year, you may realize that things are going more smoothly between you and your child. He is smiling more and screaming less;

he actually says "Yes" once in a while! He is much more cooperative in small ways—holding out his arms to be dressed, or even
closing the back door without being told. The revolution is over;
your child has lived through the struggle to separate from you and
establish his own identity. He now realizes that he can endure
being parted from you for a while, because he knows from long
experience that you love him and will not desert him. Best of all,
he can talk to you, which makes life *so* much easier. He can tell
you what he wants and why he's crying and maybe a little of what
he's thinking about. For he *is* thinking now—you see him sitting
quietly, staring out into space, reflecting on his own private
thoughts. Sometimes he comes out with questions that give you
a clue to his reflections.

"Why don't ladies have beards?"

"Will there still be bees when I grow up?"

"Mommy, when you were little, were you a boy or a girl?"

When you answer, try to do it simply, at the level of the child's
question, but expand his knowledge a little. Ladies don't have
beards because they are different from men. Can he think of any
other ways in which ladies are different from men? Get him to
notice the difference in voices, in strength, in body parts, and
most important, in the ability to bear children. (The chances are
that this is what he really wants to know; most children at this
age are very much interested in sex differences.) Stretch his mind
a little, and help him to note similarities and differences, and put
them into words. A lot of language development takes place
during this third year, and you are the child's best model. Don't
worry if he stutters a little. He's thinking faster now, and the
words come tumbling out before he has time to monitor them.
Occasionally you might ask him to repeat something slowly—you
didn't quite understand him. But don't draw attention to his
speech or show anxiety; you can create a stuttering problem
where, most likely, none exists. Just be thankful that your child

is now a delightful human being who can share his thoughts with you.

TOYS AND GAMES

What can you play with the child who is no longer a baby? Many of the things you have already been doing can be carried out in more complex ways. Your child can take a more active part in weighing, measuring, pouring, and cooking, especially since you can now explain to him what the end result will be. You are teaching him to look ahead to a goal and to think about different ways of achieving the same end. ("Shall we scramble the eggs with a fork or with a beater?")

Once the child can talk, there are all sorts of games you can play with him to help him develop sensory differentiation. You can fill opaque containers with a variety of materials—sand, pebbles, beans, screws—shake them, and ask the child to guess what's in them. Then ask him to arrange them according to volume of noise. I use inexpensive plastic salt and pepper shakers for this. The containers should be the same, so the level of noise depends on what is inside them, but be sure they are securely closed so the child doesn't get beans up his nose or pebbles in his ears. If you have a tape recorder, you can record a variety of sounds such as doorbells, a clock, familiar voices, a telephone, or a washing machine. Ask the child to identify them and see how many he can guess correctly. A "feely bag" is lots of fun; any paper bag will do. Put in several different objects such as a cold cucumber, a toothbrush, a lemon, and a spoon. Hold the bag closed at the top, with just enough room for the child to get his hand in, but not to see inside. Ask him to describe what he feels before he guesses what it is. This helps him to abstract qualities like *cold, rough,* and *squishy* from the objects themselves, and to develop the vocabulary to describe them.

Children at this age are often interested in magnets. There are large ones available, but the little ones for use on refrigerator doors always entertain Jeffrey. A magnifying glass also provides a new kind of visual experience. Let your child try looking at a fuzzy caterpillar, or the palm of his own hand in contrast to yours. A little flashlight provides hours of fun and develops visual tracking. Stringing large wooden beads fosters finger dexterity and can be used to promote ideas about things in a series. When a child has mastered the stringing itself, you can ask him to copy a simple series of beads which you make. This forces him to notice the one-to-one correspondence of three round beads in different colors, for example. Gradually you can make the patterns harder: a red circle, a green square, and a blue cube; or three small and two large beads. Then slide a row of three different-colored beads on a wire through an empty toilet paper tube and see if your child can tell you which bead will come out first at the far end. To do this successfully, he has to hold a memory image of the three beads in his head and not just name the last bead he saw disappear.

By the third year children love to imitate. You can play simplified versions of "Simon says" or "Follow the leader," depending on their language level. Finger play comes into its own, with "Ten little Indians," "This old man," and "Here's the church and here's the steeple." Your child is listening better now, and will enjoy songs, nursery rhymes, and stories. Picture books have been important from about eight months, but now the child can understand simple narratives and loves to hear them over and over again. In spite of the temptations of television, there is no substitute for a child's being read to by his parents. Study after study has shown that being read to is the most important foundation for reading success in school. The child enjoys and values reading because his parents do, and he comes to school with a vocabulary and background of knowledge into which he can assimilate the new skills he learns in the primary grades.

Now is the time when you may want to invest in a good set of blocks. Wooden blocks of various shapes encourage construction of all kinds. Putting them away, children learn to notice differences in size and shape, and to classify them accordingly. For almost-threes, an easel for drawing and painting is desirable, although fingerpainting can be done on a table covered with newspapers. Large crayons or Magic Markers fit best in small hands and can be used to scribble on junk mail and odds and ends of paper. Clay is a favorite medium which encourages creative sculpting as well as all kinds of delightful sensory experimentation. A mechanically interested child can run a sturdy children's record player and can distinguish his favorite records long before he can read their labels. Children at this age notice small details and can identify trademarks or a torn label.

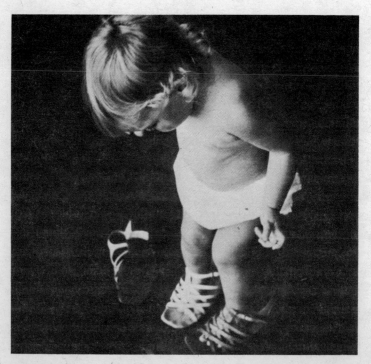

Much of the child's play may be of the make-believe variety. You will want to keep a box of "dress-up" clothes—high-heeled shoes, junk jewelry, old pocketbooks, cowboy and fireman hats, a gun and holster, a pair of boots, an old football helmet, or whatever else your attic holds. You can buy a heavy fiberboard playhouse, but my children were very happy with a bridge table over which I draped an old blanket. That became the scene of many a fantasy tale—from "playing house" to "war between the planets." A puppet theater can be made out of an appliance packing carton, with puppets fashioned out of stuffed stockings or paper bags stapled to sticks, with faces painted on them.

If your child and his friends (or siblings) are original and creative in their fantasy play, they will not need or want any help from you. However, you can often help them to get started by saying something like, "Why don't you make believe you're firefighters today? Your wagon could be the fire truck." You can always provide siren noises as you work elsewhere, and give the game a nudge in a new direction if it becomes too stereotyped. Trips to the zoo, the post office, or a construction site provide material for fantasy replays, as do visits to the airport, a train station, or the circus. Dolls can take all sorts of roles in these imaginary games, particularly if they are not too highly structured and explicitly dressed. I have already said that simple, adaptable toys are preferable for young children—plain, wooden blocks and sturdy, not too ornamental dolls. Boys can have dolls, too. They need soft and snuggly toys just as much as girls do, and the modern nonsexist attitude toward toys works both ways. Later, when they are four or five, children will want highly realistic, miniature copies of their world: dollhouses and tiny sets of dishes, service stations, trucks, and firehouses, complete to the smallest detail. But while they are this young let us encourage them to give free reign to creative imagination through simple, unstructured materials that are adaptable to many play situations.

CHAPTER 8

Play and Fantasy

Play is the chief occupation of children. It is just as important to them as a job or a profession is to their parents. In their play, children prepare themselves to cope with the world of reality: practicing motor skills, learning to discipline themselves in accordance with social rules, imitating adult roles, and reconstructing the events of their lives in their imaginations. The old saying "All work and no play makes Jack a dull boy" is literally true, as we shall find when we delve into the relationship between play and cognitive development.

Piaget became interested in children's play during his early years in Geneva. He collected more than a thousand observations of children's play in their homes, at school (particularly at the Maison des Petits), and on the street. One pictures him as a tall young man, down on his knees in the dirt, playing marbles with little boys in order to learn their understanding of the rules of the game.

"You must show me how to play," he said. "When I was little I used to play a lot, but now I've quite forgotten how. . . . You teach me the rules and I'll play with you."

Then came the questions. Have people always played as they do today? Where do rules come from? Who made them up? Could they be changed? What does it mean to "play fair"? Piaget found that by school age the children of Geneva regarded rules as sacred and unchangeable, invented by their fathers, God, or "the gentlemen of the Town Council." He came to the conclusion that games with rules such as hopscotch or marbles are essentially social, and lead to increased adaptation to the rules of society. They are at the opposite extreme from make-believe games in which objects are symbols for something quite different, existing only in the child's imagination. In such make-believe play the child is preoccupied with his own fantasy and is not concerned

with conforming to the demands of reality. The symbols he uses may be easy to identify, or very remote from reality. For example, Lucienne at 1;7 used a box to drink from. She made all the motions of sipping and swallowing, then passed the box around in an obvious attempt to share her "drink" with everyone present. But Jacqueline at 1;11 used a box in a different way; she slid a shell along the side and said, "Cat on a wall." Without her explanation, no one could have guessed that the box represented the top of a brick wall on which she had recently seen a cat walking.

In studying the evolution of children's play, Piaget concluded that there are three main categories of play. The first includes *practice games* such as throwing balls, pitching pebbles, stringing beads, or building with blocks. These grow out of the repetitive

activities of the sensory-motor period, and their function seems to be simply to improve motor skills. Out of them may develop *symbolic games* in which the blocks may represent a castle inhabited by an imaginary monster. (If the interest in the block building is more on construction, however, as in making an elaborate tower, then this is not so much a game as a constructive activity; it merges imperceptibly into the practical skills required in adult life.) The last to evolve are *games with rules* that depend on adherence to a social consensus of opinion. Such games may provide the explanation of what happens to children's play in later life; it dies out in favor of socialized games such as baseball, some of which persist into adulthood.

How does play develop in the life of a baby? Like imitation, its roots lie deep in the sensory-motor period. In its early stages, play is difficult to distinguish from ordinary adaptive behavior, since all activity in the first few months consists of repeating newly organized schemas over and over until they are mastered. However, Piaget points out that when an infant is learning a new behavior, he often has a very serious, intense expression and concentrates on his goal with great interest. Once he has mastered the new behavior he may repeat it many times with "ever-increasing enjoyment." This happy, relaxed activity just for the fun of it is for Piaget the hallmark of play as opposed to the child's "work" of accommodating to objective reality. Play develops slowly, but emerges as an observable entity in the latter half of the first year. For example, Laurent at seven months was learning to push aside an obstacle, which in this case was his father's hand, in order to reach a toy. He became more interested in the contest with his father than in the toy; pushing aside Piaget's hand, he burst into laughter and forgot all about the toy he had been trying to reach. His interest here was transferred from the goal of his action to the action itself, and what had been an intentional activity suddenly became a joyous game.

During Stage 5, as we have seen, the child characteristically varies familiar behavior patterns in order to observe different results. But sometimes, says Piaget, the child combines unrelated actions and repeats them until they become a ritualized game. He describes Jacqueline who, at a year old, was holding her hair with her right hand during her bath. Her hand, being wet, slipped and struck the water with a splash. This produced an interesting new experience, which Jacqueline immediately repeated. She varied the height and the position of her hand on her hair, but during succeeding days this behavior pattern was repeated with consistent regularity. Once Jacqueline struck the water as soon as she was put in the bath, then suddenly stopped and put her hands up to her hair, thus renewing her familiar game. Such behaviors are not adapted to external circumstances, but are repeated just for fun.

During the second year Piaget describes the emergence of true

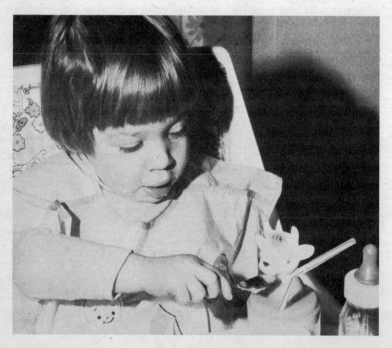

make-believe or *symbolic play*, in which an object becomes the symbol for something else which it may resemble only remotely. Jacqueline at 1;3 saw a fringed cloth whose edges reminded her of her pillow. She lay down and pretended to go to sleep, laughing all the time. Five months later she pretended to eat a piece of paper, saying, "Very nice." Before his second birthday Christopher, like many little boys, was pushing blocks around the floor and making "rrm rrm" car noises. But a few months later he suddenly ran out of the living room for no apparent reason and came back with one of those scrapers for cleaning ice and snow off car windshields. He pointed the rubber end of the scraper around the living room, making a long-drawn-out "ssshh" sound, and it suddenly dawned on me that he was pretending to spray with a hose. When I said, "Are you a fireman?" he grinned at me and nodded. One of Church's subjects in *Three Babies* was playing make-believe games by fourteen months. She would eat imaginary food or put a kitchen pot on her head and laughingly say, "Hat!"

So we see that by the end of the sensory-motor period, the elements of make-believe are clearly discernible in the child's play. He is treating objects *as if* they were something else; this "as if" behavior is what characterizes make-believe play. What the objects represent may be fairly obvious or quite distorted. The point is that the child is using symbols instead of the actual things he is thinking about. In so doing, he is functioning at the internalized level of *thought*, rather than at the sensory-motor level of external *activity*.

Between the ages of two and four symbolic play is at its peak. The child begins, according to Piaget, by projecting the earliest symbolic schemas onto new objects. Jacqueline moved from pretending she was asleep to making her dog and her bear go to sleep. Lucienne pretended to telephone, then she made her doll telephone, and finally she used all kinds of symbols, such as a leaf, instead of a real receiver. In such games, says Piaget, the child is reproducing his *own* actions just for the fun of it, and sometimes to show off for other people. But he soon moves to reproducing *other* people's looks or actions, or making his toys reproduce his own. Thus, Jacqueline at two moved her finger along the table and said, "Finger walking . . . horse trotting." At the same age Lucienne made believe she was the postman or her godmother; at four she was a belfry.

> At 4;3, L. standing at my side quite still, imitated the sound of bells. I asked her to stop, but she went on. I then put my hand over her mouth. She pushed me away, angrily, but still keeping very straight and said: *"Don't. I'm a church."*

There is a special kind of play which involves doing in make-believe what is forbidden in reality. Piaget calls this *compensatory play*. He describes Jacqueline at 2;4 going through the motions of pouring water with an empty cup after she had been forbidden to play in the real washtub. At 2;7 she wanted to carry Lucienne, who was then a newborn baby. When her mother told her she could not carry the baby yet, Jacqueline folded her arms and announced that she had the baby—there were two babies. Then she rocked and talked to the imaginary baby, and even said she *was* the baby when she was scolded for screaming with temper, thus excusing her behavior. Closely allied to this is the type of play in which children act out some of the traumas of childhood such as death or accidents. By reliving them in fantasy, they reduce their feelings of terror surrounding these situations, and thus make them more tolerable. This is the usual explanation of why children enjoy horror movies on TV. They know the scene is not real, that they can turn it off at will, so they are able to cope with the horror and master their own fear in slow degrees. In the following observation Jacqueline shows how a child acts out and learns to live with the unpleasant realities of life.

At 3;11(21) J. was impressed by the sight of a dead duck which had been plucked and put on the kitchen table. The next day I found J. lying motionless on the sofa in my study, her arms pressed against her body and her legs bent: "What are you doing, J.? Have you a pain? Are you ill? *No, I'm the dead duck.*"

This kind of role playing is useful to children because it helps them understand strange or scary experiences. Here Jacqueline was trying to comprehend through her stiff little body what it must feel like to be dead. Parents can often help children prepare for fearful situations such as surgery by playing "doctor" with them, or using dolls to represent family situations which may be causing stress. I remember one little girl who "played house" very

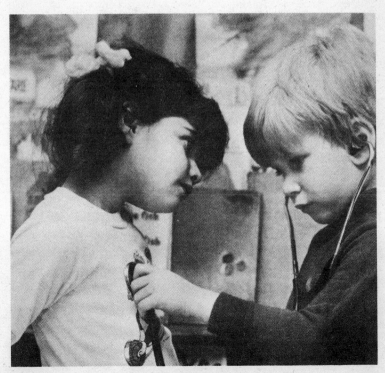

nicely with me right after her new baby brother was born. She put
the baby doll in a tiny crib near the mother's bed "so she can take
care of it." Then, watching me sideways, she took the baby out
of the crib and threw it in the toilet.

"You'd really like to get rid of that baby, wouldn't you?" I
asked.

She nodded, relieved that I got the message.

"Babies can be an awful nuisance," I went on. "They keep your
mommy busy so she can't play with you very much."

"And they cry at night and wake me up," complained the child.

"But pretty soon they get bigger and you can play with them,"
I said cheerfully. "When your brother gets a little bigger, your
mommy might let you take him for a ride in the carriage."

The little girl heaved a sigh; then she retrieved the baby doll
from the toilet and put it in a miniature doll carriage. Her anger
had been understood, not condemned, and now it seemed to have
evaporated.

It is during the third year that the child's fantasy play is most
far-fetched and his view of reality most distorted. This is probably
because he is still bound up in egocentric feelings and has so many
new adjustments to make in such a short time. At this period of
his life the child is subjected to more parental demands than at
any other time. Constantly he hears, "No, no," "Don't touch,"
"Stay out of the street," "Don't get dirty," "Time for bed." He
must be toilet-trained, learn to talk correctly, adapt to a time
schedule, and acquire proper table manners. His daily life is polar-
ized around his efforts to adapt to reality and thus please his
parents, and his efforts to escape from these demands and satisfy
the needs of his own emerging ego. But gradually, as he becomes
more adjusted to the world around him, parental pressures upon
him decrease and his need to escape into the world of make-
believe becomes less urgent. He is learning to express himself
better in words; he is also more aware of how events follow each

other in time and space. Slowly his stories become more realistic and coherent; in time his fantasy play is almost indistinguishable from the events of his everyday life.

Do children really believe in their own fantasies? Piaget feels that it depends on the age of the child. While children very early make the distinction between what's real and what's "pretend," they refuse to allow adults or ordinary events to interfere with the enjoyment of their own private world of make-believe. The child is aware that his fantasies are not real for other people, but for him, says Piaget, ". . . it is a question which does not arise."

In reading Piaget, one realizes the meaning and importance of symbolic play in the life of a child. It is an intermediate step between the world of things directly experienced and the world

of thought. As I have stressed before in talking about toys, the more the child plays with things that suggest many uses, the more he is stimulated to think of alternatives. Slowly his rigid, concrete thinking becomes flexible and creative. He comes up with a dozen different uses for the same thing. A little red wagon can be a truck, a fire engine, a train, an ambulance, a lunar module. The child experiments in his play, trying out different roles, costumes, and speech patterns. At around age three his ideas may be illogical and distorted, but by four or five he will be more and more attuned to the world of reality. (*That* is the time when he wants toys that are miniatures of real life: tiny cars, a dollhouse, a farmhouse with all the animals.) His flights into fantasy will become "interiorized," as Piaget puts it, to be expressed in day-dreams and sometimes in drawings. But the originality and flexibility of thought which they engender will enrich developing intellectual interests for the rest of his life. In the words of Piaget, "Creative imagination . . . does not diminish with age but . . . is gradually reintegrated in intelligence, which is thereby correspondingly broadened."

Piaget's emphasis on the importance of symbolic play has stimulated a good deal of research among cognitive psychologists. Dr. Jerome Singer of Yale has supervised and published considerable work on the creative functions of make-believe play and day-dreaming. He concludes that the ability to fantasize helps children explore different possibilities, endure boredom, control aggressive impulses, and increase storytelling skills. It is a creative, cognitive ability which makes life richer for all of us, and which should be encouraged in childhood. He and his wife Dr. Dorothy Singer have conducted studies showing that young children pick up the skill of making believe much more readily if they have an adult model to imitate. Observing nursery school children, they found that the greatest interest in spontaneous make-believe play came when the children's teacher engaged in make-believe games and encouraged them to do likewise. To help teachers and parents of small children, the Singers have put together a book full of imaginative games, songs, and simple plays, as well as suggestions for the constructive use of television. In it they state that "while the capacity for fantasy or pretending is inherent in all reasonably normal human beings, the degree to which it is used by children depends to a large extent on whether parents or other adults have fostered it."

I remember the mother of a little girl who was the most imaginative of the "high fantasy" children in a research project. She told me that every summer she and her husband took their family to their vacation cottage, which had a mossy path through the woods to the lake where they went swimming.

"We always looked for the leprechaun who lived in a mossy green house under the rocks," she said.

"Did the children believe you?" I asked.

"Does it matter?" she replied. "At least they were stretching their minds and their imaginations, looking for what *might* be, and not just for what was."

CHAPTER 9

The Development of Language

The last and most important of the symbolic functions to appear is that of language. Despite what we are now learning about chimpanzees and dolphins, language appears to be exclusively a human achievement. The ability to talk to others opens up a whole new universe for mankind; we can communicate emotions, work out compromises, learn from the past, and plan for the future. A common language is what rescues children from egocentricity and magic, and makes their world predictable.

Children usually begin to talk during the second year. Some are precocious and say their first words sooner; others are slower and more deliberate. I know one bright little girl whose mother was concerned because the child made no effort to talk until she was well past two. Her first words, however, dumfounded her mother. One day, out of a clear blue sky, the little girl said, "Please may I have some more M & M's?"

Much of the material in this chapter derives from a series of lectures in developmental psycholinguistics given by Dr. Hermine Sinclair at the University of Geneva, which I was privileged to attend. I wish to acknowledge my great indebtedness to her, and to thank Laurie Miller, who helped me translate the French lecture notes into English.

Children tend to talk sooner if they are talked *to*. They imitate and respond to conversation directed to them, just as they do to smiling and cooing. Children who are deprived of being talked to may develop very late or very poor speech. I once had a little boy referred to me professionally because his kindergarten teacher couldn't understand a word he said. It turned out that his mother had been quite ill after he was born and that he had spent most of his first two years alone in his room with only the TV for company. Hearing the TV and radio is not enough; to babies they represent a meaningless Babel of sound. Studies have shown that babies in middle-class families develop language sooner than those in economically deprived homes. In the latter there is constant noise from the media, and from people talking around but not *to* the baby. The kind of intimate personal communication that goes on in "one-to-one conversations" between parent and child appears to be the most meaningful introduction to language.

Sometimes, however, children seem to be slow in talking because there is no need for them to make the effort. Parents may anticipate their every wish; in a big family the older children may understand a baby's gestures so well that he rarely needs to use words. But most babies begin to talk somewhere between one and a half to two years of age, as the sensory-motor period of development draws to a close.

According to Piaget, language appears along with the other symbolic functions such as deferred imitation and make-believe play. Like them, it has its roots in sensory-motor intelligence, in all the learning which precedes the ability to represent physical reality in mental images. When the toddler says, "Where doggie go?" it means that he knows his dog has an independent existence, he retains a mental image of the absent dog, and he can supply the correct word for it. Pictures, gestures, and images resemble in some way the objects they represent; words do not. Language is really an arbitrary "sign system"; our society has agreed that "dog" is the word for a certain class of animals, whereas the French have agreed on "chien" and the Japanese on "inu." The child learns the sign symbols of his mother tongue just as he learns that red means "stop" and green means "go."

Long before the child is capable of dealing with socialized sign symbols, he is learning to communicate and to express himself. This prelanguage period begins at birth with crying, which is one of the reflex responses of the newborn. The birth cry is soon modified to express different needs. Wolff has shown experimentally that experienced mothers can tell from listening to a baby's cry whether he is hungry, or angry, or in pain. This is the language of discomfort; its opposite also develops very early. The baby smiles and coos when he is comfortable and happy. When the mother smiles and coos back at him, we have the beginnings of language—one person making sounds to which another responds.

At around a month the baby begins to babble. First he makes a series of vowel sounds, with consonants gradually added. Soon he is repeating strings of consonant-vowel sounds over and over, playing with them much as he plays with his fingers and toes. This circular repetition of sounds is similar to the motor activity of the early sensory-motor stages; by making sounds the baby stimulates himself to make more sounds. Soon he passes from repeating sounds for the sake of hearing them to discovering new sounds which he adds to his repertoire. This may be referred to as the "goo-goo" stage, but if you listen carefully, you will hear the baby experimenting with an increasingly complex and diversified pattern of consonant-vowel combinations. These are varied according to pitch, rhythm, and stress. They may even end with a rising inflection, as if the baby were asking a question. For example:

> adididyda
> affú áffu apupu
> álala alála ábabbab abábba baba?

As teeth appear and the baby gains control over the muscles of his lips, tongue, and palate, he can produce a greater variety of sounds. When he begins to sit up, at about six months, it is easier for him to move his lips and also to watch the lips of others. We begin to hear *p, b, m;* then *f* and *s;* then *o, oo,* and *ee.* The baby hears them, too; he is enjoying the feedback from the sounds he is making, and is trying to imitate those that other people make to him. Piaget describes Jacqueline, who at nearly seven months invented a new sound by putting her tongue between her teeth. The sound came out something like *pfs.* Her mother imitated it, and Jacqueline, laughing delightedly, repeated it. This went on for several weeks, after which either her father or her mother could say *pfs* and Jacqueline would imitate them.

Up to about eight months of age, as each baby experiments with his vocal apparatus, he produces an enormous diversity of sounds. These sounds are universally heard in babies all over the world. After about eight months, however, the baby begins to

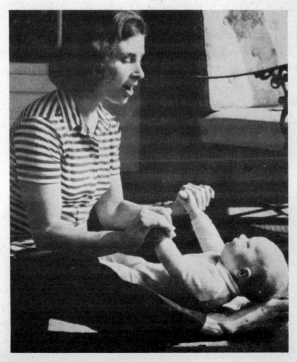

stop making the sounds which he doesn't hear from the people around him. Instead he concentrates on the sounds that he hears his parents make, and begins to assimilate the melody of his mother tongue. This is why it is so important to talk to your baby from the very beginning, and encourage him to talk to you. It is interesting to note that deaf children also go through this universal babbling stage, but do not develop beyond it. Their babbling gradually fades away, presumably because they do not hear the feedback that would guide them toward developing language.

The baby's first words are usually, though not always, *mama* and *papa* or *dada*. The psycholinguist M. M. Lewis says there are six repetitive nursery words which appear throughout the world in broadly the same sound patterns—the three mentioned above, plus *nana, baba,* and *tata. Mama* (or *maman* in French) arises naturally out of the child's sucking noises *(mmm)* and is associated with the presence of the mother during nursing, that most pleasurable of activities. Imagine a contented baby, smacking his lips after a satisfying meal, and producing a sound like *mamamama.* Then picture his delighted mother exclaiming, "He said *Mama!*" as she hugs and fondles the baby. With all the subsequent reinforcement ("Listen, he can say *Mama!* Say *Mama* for Daddy!") the child soon learns that saying *Mama* effectively brings him food, comfort, and help when he needs it, as well as large doses of emotional response.

Along with these feeling-laden words *mama* and *dada*, the child is learning the names of many other things in his environment. His first attempts may be approximations that only a parent could understand—*buh* for *bug* or *bottle, gah* for *car, pay* for *plane.* Christopher had a hard time with initial *s* sounds; *snow* was *no, snake* was *nake, stop* was *tah.* Despite the difficulties, the toddler struggles on, constantly asking, "Whaddat?" and reproducing as best he can the name of everything that interests him. To him words are magic; they make things happen. To know the names of things, as we have said before, is to have power over them, and the child at this stage is filled with a sense of magic omnipotence.

There is a big difference between expressive language, which we are talking about here, and receptive language or understanding, which the child achieves much earlier. Long before he uses words, the baby can understand and respond to requests such as "Show me your nose," "Give Mummy the spoon," or "Go get your shoes." At about a year old, Chris was trying to push down the pegs in a pounding bench with his fingers. It was rough going, and finally I said to him, "Why don't you use the hammer, Chris?" I had no idea whether he knew the word "hammer" or not. He looked at me, and then without hesitation he turned around, picked up the hammer from the floor behind him, and followed my suggestion with vigor.

The names of household objects are learned most easily during the rituals of meal and bath times, when the same terms are regularly used by the same person for the same things. *Spoon, cup, plate, eat, drink, sponge, duck, wash,* and *soap* are words often used in such a way that the child begins to see the relationship between the label and the object or action named. Other frequently repeated phrases such as "Time for bed," or "Daddy's coming!" give the child a sense of the temporal continuity of events. He feels comfortable in a familiar setting, with a mother who understands his attempts to approximate her speech. I am certain that one contributing factor to the toddler's fear of strangers is the problem of not being understood. The child says something his mother would understand perfectly, and finds himself facing a blank wall or, even worse, a complete misinterpretation. One well-meaning grandmother I know was giving her year-old granddaughter her supper. She was just opening the refrigerator when the little girl cried "Cockapoo!" Only the last syllable registered in the grandmother's mind; she quickly took the child out of her high chair and rushed her upstairs to the bathroom. The child sat on her potty seat for quite a while, but nothing happened. Finally the grandmother took her back to the kitchen to finish her supper. She put the child in her high chair and went back to the refrigerator. Again the child shouted "Cockapoo!" The grandmother went through the whole routine a second time with no greater success. When the mother came home and heard the recital of these events, she burst out laughing. "Cockapoo," she explained, "means chocolate pudding. Annie knows I keep it in the refrigerator."

Around the time a child learns to use single words, he usually develops a whole new flow of speech. This is a kind of gibberish that sounds remarkably like language, with all its rhythms and intonations, and with just enough real words thrown in to make it convincing. Sometimes called "expressive jargon," it sounds like the double-talk one hears from a good comedian. You may be horrified someday to hear your child mimicking accurately your panic or fury in moments of emotional stress. The words may not

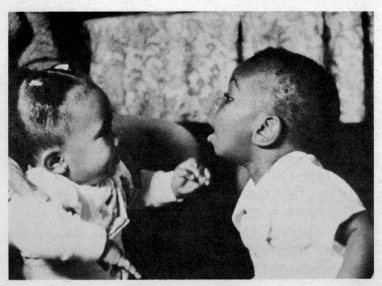

be there, but the angry hysterical tones are very clear. Children will also imitate over and over again phrases which catch their attention. My daughter once stepped on the cat and said, "Sorry, Coco." That was all she heard from Chris for the rest of the morning! A few months later, when he was noticing traffic signs, he asked about a sign that said DON'T WALK. For three blocks thereafter, Christopher trotted beside me, repeating, "Don't walk," in a very serious tone. Whenever the buzzer sounded in my car, he announced: "Fasten seat belts," the words that lit up on a red panel.

The beginnings of real communication, which are neither babbling nor jargon, emerge somewhere around one and a half or two, toward the end of the sensory-motor period. These are usually one or two words used with gestures or expressions to signify the meaning of a whole sentence.

"Eat!"—I want to eat, or You eat it.

"Out!"—I want to go out, or Get out of here (the bathroom).

"Boom!"—Something fell down.

"Boom bell"—Someone is ringing the doorbell.

"Mummy hair"—Mummy's hair, or Mummy cut her hair.

"Daddy car"—Daddy's car, or Daddy is in his car.

"Mommy sock"—Child is putting on Mother's sock, or Mother is putting a sock on the child.

This early stage of speech leaves out all nonessential words (pronouns, prepositions, articles) and concentrates on nouns and verbs. It has the terseness of a telegram, and therefore has been called "telegraphic speech." It seems to be a universal stage; at least it has been found in studies of Finnish, Hebrew, Chinese, Russian, French, and Korean children. This stage is also interesting because the child creates words which do not exist in his native language, but are more grammatically regular than those that do. "Mommy singed" is more regular than "sang"; "fire-mans" and "tooths" are more logical than irregular plurals. Negatives present a problem in English. A child might start with "not want" and progress to "don't want some," "don't want none," and finally to "don't want any." I know a little girl who has her whole family saying, "I don't gots none." In examples like these we see how the child, in learning to speak, passes through the following stages: (1) active imitation, (2) attempts to apply the rules of grammar, (3) recognition of exceptions to the rules. For example, in learning to use the term "feet" the child may go through the following progression:

$$feet \longrightarrow foots \longrightarrow feets \longrightarrow feet$$

The first "feet" reflects only imitation, whereas the last one shows recognition of an exception to the rule that plurals are formed by adding *s*.

In these early one- or two-word utterances (and the two words are often lumped together as one, like "Awgone" or "Whad-dat?") we observe the child's attempts to assimilate the correct labels to his mental schema, and to accommodate his speech to the rules of his native tongue. From the ease with which he acquires the structures of language, it becomes apparent that the development of language and thought are inextricably entwined. The child learns to manipulate an arbitrary sign-symbol system and adapt it to rules of syntax which are often less than logical. In fact, we see the child's logic struggling against the irregularities of grammar, and organizing speech into transposed structures which could not have been imitated because they have not been heard. If a harassed mother says to her daughter, "Go tell Daddy I need him," the child does not repeat to her father, "I need him." She translates the message into "Mommy needs you," a miracle of logical recomposition.

There are other ways in which the development of language

and thought are reflected in each other. In Chapter 7 we discussed the fuzzy, global, overextended preconcepts of the young
child, in which all slugs are "that slug again" and all men are
"Daddy." The understanding of words develops in much the
same way. At 1;1 Jacqueline used the sound *tch tch* to imitate a
passing train, as many children do. But later she used it in connection with all kinds of vehicles, and also with anything that appeared and disappeared like the train. By 1;6 she had become well
aware that her grandfather, whom she called "Panana," would do
whatever her little heart desired. She began to say "panana" not
only to call him, but whenever she wanted anything, and even
when she simply wanted to be amused. Children have always
overextended their first words in a way that is different from
adults. It is reported that Darwin's son said "quack" to refer to
a duck, and then to water, then to birds and insects as well as to
other liquids. Later on he saw an eagle on a French coin; thereafter coins were called "quack" as well. We can learn a good deal
about how a child thinks by his departure from adult classifications. We see that this boy is assimilating new situations (eagles
on a coin) to past experience (ducks and other birds). But his
experience is limited, and so is his logic. As both increase, the
child will learn to differentiate more precisely, and to define the
meanings of his words more exactly. For example, ducks (or
"quacks") are birds, but not all birds are ducks. The growth of
language and the growth of thought influence each other mutu-
ally.

As the child moves into his third year his vocabulary is growing
enormously. Both his language and his grammar are increasing in
complexity. Longer sentences of from three to seven words now
appear. Prepositions such as *in* or *on* are used, along with an
occasional article. Verbs are combined with *am, is,* or *are.* Plurals
and possessives are heard, along with past tenses, even though
they may still be ungrammatically "regular." "All these," writes

Roger Brown, "like an intricate sort of ivy, begin to grow up between and upon the major construction blocks, the nouns and verbs." Questions appear more frequently and in more complex form. "Whaddat?" gives way to *why* and *when* questions such as "Why the dog won't eat?"

This is the ideal time for learning a second language. Young children adapting to a foreign tongue seem to pick up the structure of a second language as quickly as they do those of their own. Professor Hermine Sinclair of the University of Geneva tells the story of a multilingual child whose father was an American diplomat living abroad. The little girl's mother was French, the maid was Belgian, the cook was German, and the chauffeur was Italian. The child grew up accepting it as a fact of life that every person in the world had a special language of his own!

Children of around three years of age are likely to garble long words, reversing the syllables as in *aminals* and *pasghetti*. The child of a psychologist I know calls his toy motorcycle a "psychomotor." Another tendency of this age is to clump words together, so that *allofus* becomes one word, as do *potsnpans*. It is not only the young who pray, "Our Father, whartnheavn...."

Pronouns provide another problem for young children. *Me* and *mine* appear very early, but the subjective pronoun *I* is not mastered until later. It is hard to explain to children when they should use *I*. When Chris was just past two, I was putting him to bed at my house where he was visiting overnight. First I had to run downstairs for a diaper, and then for a bottle, and then again for his security blanket. The following exchange took place between Chris and his weary grandmother:

> *Grandma:* You make me run up and down!
> *Chris:* Me make you run up and down.
> *Grandma:* No, you say, "I make you run up and down."
> *Chris:* You make you run up and down!

Parents do not usually try to correct their children's grammar; they will frequently correct pronunciation or factual errors, but they are wise enough to know that the grammar will straighten itself out in time. Like the parents whose child announced, "Mummy isn't a boy. He's a girl!" they are delighted that at least the facts are understood.

The most effective way of teaching language is to answer children's questions in correct English and elaborate on their primitive sentences as I heard this mother do for her two-year-old daughter.

Child: Where kitty is?
Mother: Where is your kitty? I don't know.
Child: Where her go?
Mother: Where did she go? Maybe she went under the sofa.

Child (looking): Her no dere.

Mother: She's not there? Maybe she's behind the big chair.

Child: Here kitty is! Annie kitty!

Mother: Here is Annie's kitty! She is behind the big chair.

This is the way a child learns language, in the context of family life. The parents act as models, guiding the child in the elaboration of his language and the improvement of his grammar. It is sometimes a temptation to imitate baby talk, and every family has its favorite expressions, but this tends to perpetuate the child's immature speech. I knew a little girl who delighted in showing her father the "pitty lellow fodders." Instead of elaborating correctly for her by saying, "No, pretty yellow flowers," he imitated her, until one fine day she haughtily corrected *him.* "Not fodders, Daddy," she said, "fwowows!" By gradual approximations she approached the correct pronunciation. As I have mentioned, Christopher had difficulty in sounding the initial *s* on words beginning with two consonants (i.e., snapper), but he could hear the difference if someone else left out the *s*. One summer day he was helping his grandfather move the lawn sprinkler, which his grandfather, imitating him, referred to as the "prinkler." Chris immediately corrected him. "Not prinkler, Grandpa," he said, "it's a *prinkler!*" His ear was more accurate than his tongue.

By the time a child is three he probably has a vocabulary of about a thousand words. His language is imaginative and colorful, expressing the quicksilver of his logic. Listen carefully, and you may learn that a bald man has a "barefoot head," or that the father of a grasshopper is a "daddyhopper." You may hear phrases such as "softy sand," "a dusky-dusky voice," or "balloony legs." For the language of a child is as fresh and vivid as his fantasies. If your child talks to himself before falling asleep, you may want to put a tape recorder under his bed. In any event, listen to him with ears sharp enough to hear not only his words but the emotions underlying them. If you are lucky, you may share a moment of poetry such as this:

It's summer—warm! And it will rain. And blow down wind. And there will be a stor-r-rm! And there will be snowdrops in my mother's garden. And the birds stayed up all night.

CHAPTER 10

Looking Ahead

Your child is three years old, and it's time to stop and take stock of his development. If all has gone well, that tiny, dependent infant of yours has grown into a cheerful, cooperative, independent child who says "Sure," instead of "No," when you ask him to do something. He is alert, inventive, and interested in many things; his increasing questions reflect a curious and critical mind. His deepest love and trust are reserved for you, his parents, but he is capable of warm relationships with familiar adults such as grandparents, neighbors, or babysitters. He is very much interested in other children and actively seeks their company. His world is expanding, and he is eager for new experiences.

Now that this child is becoming daily more social, what lies ahead for him and for you? He needs playmates, and you may be thinking of having another baby. Or you may be considering nursery school for him. You may want to take a job. Each of these choices involves certain problems about which you will be thinking.

Many couples today are satisfied to have an only child; the

advantages of such a situation are being touted as never before. However, if you enjoy children and want to have another, a very good time to become pregnant is when your first child is close to three. If you wait much longer, it will be more difficult for him because he will be too accustomed to having all his parents' attention. If you start much sooner, you may be struggling with a new baby along with the trials of coping with a two-year-old. Having a sibling is hard on the first child—make no mistake about it. In most cases, it will only add to the problems of a two-year-old if you produce a rival at a time when he most needs your affection for himself. It will be easier on all of you if the new baby does not arrive until your first child is three or older.

If you do become pregnant, *don't* tell your child too soon; his concept of time is limited and he will only forget. When you are visibly pregnant, you might explain in very simple terms that you and Daddy are going to have a baby; that it is growing inside of your body. Then wait to see whether the child asks for more information. The level of explanation you give him depends very much on his particular level of development. A recent study by Anne Bernstein and Philip Cowan indicates that children's ideas about human reproduction pass through a predictable developmental sequence. Little children, they found, assume that babies have always existed; the question is *where?* Their three-year-old subjects replied, "You go to a baby store and buy one," or "In my mommy's tummy—it was there all the time." They conclude that children's ability to assimilate sex information is related to their level of understanding. No matter how carefully you explain procreation to your child, he will probably hear only what he is ready to hear, and will construct his own ideas about where babies come from and, later on, how they are born. Telling him too much too soon or too graphically often gives rise to unnecessary anxiety.

You will have plenty of time to prepare your child gradually for the arrival of a new baby, so let him ask you for more information when he is ready. His questions may come immediately, or after he has been mulling them over in his mind for a while. They may be very direct, or they may be disguised in veiled or symbolic language. First, see if you can discover your child's preconceived notions by asking him, "What do *you* think?" Then tell him just as much as he needs to know for his level of understanding. The baby grows inside the mother in a special place called a uterus or a womb. The uterus has a special opening which is separate from the openings for feces or urine. How does the baby get there? It grows from a tiny egg that the mother's body makes (*not* a hen's egg that she eats). What makes it start to grow? The father. How? The father's body has sperms just as the mother's body has eggs. It takes a father and a mother to make a baby. When the father's sperm and the mother's egg come together inside the mother's uterus, the baby starts to grow. It grows inside the mother's body until it is ready to be born.

Choose carefully the words you use in describing where the baby is. The phrases "in my tummy" or "in my stomach" suggest to many children that the baby is made by eating and born through excretion. Piaget quotes a child who asked about a pregnant mother, "Where is the baby now?" When her mother replied, "It is inside her," the child said, "Has she eaten it?" A child at the Maison des Petits asked her teacher, "What do mummies eat to be able to make babies?" If parents talk about sperm as seeds and about mummies having eggs, they may discover their children swallowing watermelon seeds, or being suddenly afraid to eat eggs for breakfast. Boys as well as girls sometimes become extremely constipated trying to hold onto their feces in the belief that they are "making a baby." The best thing to do, if you notice this happening, is to state in a matter-of-fact way that only grown women can have babies, not little girls or boys.

You will undoubtedly have to repeat the story several times, adding more details as the child asks more questions. There are several simple and beautifully illustrated books on the market (see Appendix B) to help you when the going gets more graphic. But don't think that reading a book with your child is any substitute for the sex education he is getting from watching his parents in their day-to-day relationship. A woman who is loving and happy, a man who is tender and protective—these are the best educators a child can have. As long as he feels free to ask about whatever he wants to know, and as long as parents are open and comfortable in their explanations, the child's questions will be appropriately answered.

It is a good idea to include the older child in your preparations for the new baby. If he is still sleeping in the crib, get him into a "big bed" of his own as soon as possible, so that he doesn't feel he is being dispossessed when the baby comes. You may see him struggling to grow up as the weeks go by. He may want to give up his bottle or refuse to wear diapers at night because he is "too big." He may also draw closer to his father, which allows his mother to separate from him and free herself for the new baby.

But in spite of all these careful preparations, your youngster may have quite a strong reaction when the newborn actually appears on the scene. He may regress, crying a lot for attention or demanding to be breast-fed. Sometimes there are surreptitious physical attacks on the baby such as pinching him or taking away his bottle. More often there are verbal assaults with dramatic suggestions for getting rid of the unwelcome rival. This at least gets the problem out in the open without any actual harm to the new baby. You can always be accepting of the older child's feelings, and simply letting him talk out his resentment may lessen it. You can also be sensitive to symbolic ways in which he expresses the emotions he is afraid to put into words—stomping on "babies" made out of clay or damaging the baby's toys in place of the living infant. If you can interpret what he is feeling as I

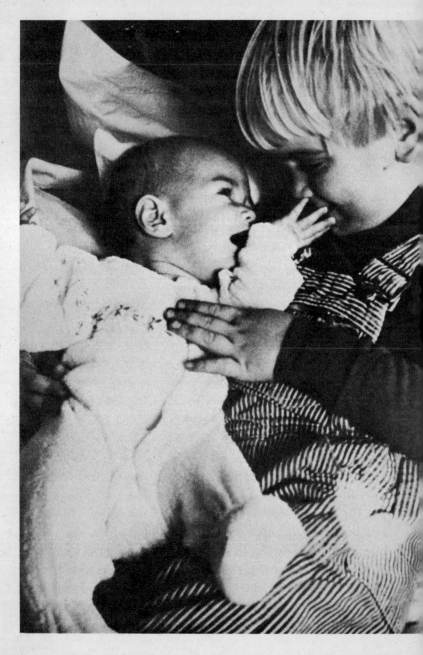

did in the example on page 152, you can relieve his anger without making him feel guilty. But it is still a bitter struggle for the firstborn to give up his special place in his parents' affections and share them with an interloper. Christopher, one morning, came into his parents' bedroom where the middle pillow on their king-size bed had always been reserved for him. When he saw two-week-old Jeffrey ensconced on *his* pillow, poor Christopher shrieked, "Get he out of there!" and ran sobbing into his own room.

In time, however, as the baby begins to laugh and chortle at the antics of the older child, he may find himself actually enjoying his little sister or brother. That doesn't necessarily mean an end to rivalry, which after all is a fact of life between siblings. As the months go by, however, their relationship will probably improve and eventually they will develop the love and concern for each other that supersede momentary squabbles and build true family solidarity.

What if, instead of having another baby, you decide to take a job? In that case, you are faced with a whole set of different problems. This is a decision that depends on many factors—what kind of job, how much you want or need it, how long you will be absent, who will care for your child, whether your husband is willing to cooperate with you. If he is, and you can get a job with hours complementary to his, you may be able to share your child's care between you. Today, some fathers are taking paternity leaves, and many mothers are on flexible employment schedules—working in a restaurant during the dinner hour, processing checks in a bank at night, or teaching evening courses. Flextime (a European plan for flexible working hours) and the four-day week are being adopted by an increasing number of companies. More and more mothers of preschool children are working part-time, but even part-time jobs require careful arrangements. There has to be dependable backup care during holidays and illnesses unless one parent can take time off for such emergencies. You may end up spending almost as much for quality child care as you can earn.

What it comes down to is a very personal decision based on your particular circumstances and your child's ability to accept your absence. In reading this book, you have seen why most children need their mothers (or at least one consistent caregiver) until they are about three. If you have devoted yourself to your child's care for three full years, you may now feel entitled to "do your own thing." You may be itching to get back your old independence, to dress with style and have an interesting job and your own income. Or you may *have* to work because you badly need the income. But it's not that easy. From now on, you are going to have to juggle your needs against your child's, and cope with the problems, both present and potential, that inevitably arise. You are going to be torn between the demands of your job and the demands of your home, pursued by the sense of guilt that haunts the working mothers of young children. It can be done, but only at a price which you need to consider carefully before making a decision.

Actually, the price is a dual one; in addition to emotional stress it includes a financial burden. The latter may be negligible if you are able to earn a substantial salary, but good nursery schools now charge from $500 to $1,000 a year, depending on location. Day care programs vary widely, both in cost and quality: some programs are well funded and provide excellent educational settings, while others are dingy or deplorable, giving only minimal custodial care. Parents considering these facilities should keep in mind the same questions that are raised later in this chapter in reference to nursery schools.

Furthermore, good preschool programs only run for three or four hours a day. It is the consensus of educators that the benefits of such programs "diminish or are even cancelled when the school day is prolonged to six hours or beyond. Most children begin to show the strain of prolonged separation from mother and home after a few hours." This means that in addition to tuition, you must consider the cost of child care after school hours if your job demands it, as well as during holidays, vacations, and illnesses. The kind of person you would like to have take care of your child may charge as much as you can earn, if in fact such a person is available to you at all. If you must settle for whomever you can get, bear in mind that children of three or four quickly pick up poor language habits; they are also highly susceptible to old wives' tales of "boogey men" and other horrors during this age of magical thinking.

This is not meant to discourage you from working if that is your choice; I am all in favor of women having satisfying jobs and careers. The problem is that our society is simply not set up to meet the needs of working mothers, particularly those of pre-school children. We need good day care programs for all income levels, and well-trained "child care professionals." There should be nurseries in plants and factories where mothers can spend their lunch hours and breaks with their children. Most important of all, there should be far more part-time jobs at which mothers can work on flexible schedules adjusted to the needs of their children. Women must put pressure on big business and the government to achieve these objectives through legislation, lobbies and women's organizations. Until such goals become reality, working mothers must be prepared for double responsibility and double stress on themselves and possibly on their marriages.

Thus the decision to work outside your home when your children are young becomes a matter of individual priorities. If your husband or parents are truly supportive, and if you can arrange an appropriate school setting and/or dependable home care, you may be able to manage a job, at least part time. If you decide it's not worth the hassle, remember that the process of rearing two children to elementary school age takes only ten to twelve years, depending on the amount of overlap between babies. That leaves most healthy women another twenty or thirty years to pursue their own careers. Only you can decide the priorities for yourself and your family.

Whether you work or not, your child is increasingly a social being who needs other children to play with. If you are at home, you may be able to join in an informal play group with two or three other mothers who share your ideas about child rearing and whose children get along with yours. The children should be close to each other in developmental level so that no one child is the bully or the scapegoat. The mothers should share common attitudes about how much mess they can tolerate in their homes, and where to draw the line between precaution and overprotection. They should agree on such policies as letting the children learn by exploring and figuring things out for themselves, and not intervening too readily in children's quarrels. Children learn more by solving their own problems. If you must intervene, try to help each child to respect the feelings and rights of others, and to understand their points of view.

I stress the point of sharing common attitudes because chil-

dren's fights can cause hard feelings between old friends. Parents remember these things much longer than their children do. But if you can talk things over together, with large doses of good humor and tolerance, it can be a satisfying experience. Mothers can learn a lot about their own children by watching how they behave in such a group. If your child is consistently the weeper, the whiner, or the bully, it tells you something about your parenting that you may not have realized.

Most such groups rotate in the mothers' homes, meeting once or twice a week for a couple of hours. You might start by having all the mothers stay with their children, and gradually cut down to two or, for short periods only, one supervising mother with another on call nearby. Sometimes mothers tend to socialize with each other; or their own children may act up when they are present. In such cases, keeping the group small enough for one mother to handle may work out better. Fathers can be a welcome addition to such groups, playing with the youngsters and adding masculine zest to their games. One group had a wonderful mailman who used to come by every day. He knew all the children by name and let them take turns delivering letters to the resident mother. You could arrange for each child to bring one favorite toy, with the understanding that he must be willing to share it and take turns with the other children. Perhaps a carton of simple, sturdy puzzles and blocks, plus some favorite books and records, could be moved from house to house. The cost of juice and crackers can be shared in the same way.

If you feel your child is mature enough for a regular nursery school setting, you and your husband will want to look over the alternatives available in your community and decide which one best suits your family's needs and whether it is worth the cost. There are books that can help you; see those listed in Appendix B. A private nursery school can be quite expensive; a cooperative nursery school will be less, but can take a lot of your time and

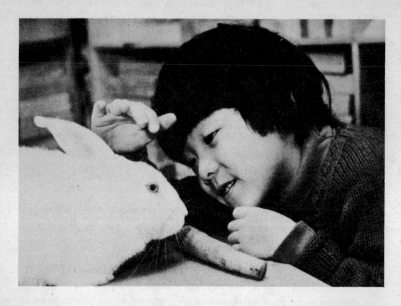

commitment. There are traditional nursery schools, Montessori schools, and a new breed of "learning centers" where the emphasis is on elaborate equipment. You will want to talk to knowledgeable people who have children in the schools you are interested in and, finally, go to visit the schools, preferably without your child.

You may encounter a good deal of reluctance to let you come and observe when the children are there (which gives you a clue to the school's attitude). But persist—say you wouldn't think of sending your child to a school you hadn't seen for yourself. Some schools have a one-way observation mirror through which you can see the children but they can't see you. If you are in a room with children, be as quiet and unobtrusive as possible. Teachers are often legitimately reluctant to have visitors who interrupt and distract the children from their activities.

When you visit a school that interests you, the first thing you will want to assess is the emotional atmosphere. Does it have a cheerful, comfortable feeling? Do the children appear to be the kind you want for your child's friends? Do they appear happily busy, or are they standing around looking irritable and bored? How many quarrels do you see, and how does the teacher handle them? How many children per teacher? For three-year-olds no more than six or eight to a trained teacher is advisable.

Next, take a look at the teachers; their role is crucial to your child's happiness and success in school. Do they look as if they truly enjoy youngsters? Are they really involved, or sitting on the sidelines waiting for trouble to start? *How* are they involved? Are they laying down rules for the children to follow, or supplying materials which the children can use to work out solutions to their own problems? According to Piaget, the good teacher does not "teach"; she is a catalyst who arranges situations which invite children to formulate their own questions and come up with their own answers. For example, she might leave a magnet on a low table along with paper clips, washers, plastic buttons, and tooth-picks. Sooner or later somebody will discover that the magnet can pick up the washers but not the buttons. This could precipitate a discussion. Why does it pick up some things and not others? How are the things it picks up alike? Can you predict what it will pick up and what it won't? These are mind-stretching exercises for small children, to be carried on only as long as they are interested.

Of course you will want to talk with the director to find out about the school's philosophy and what it expects from parents. You will probably want to ask about the teachers' qualifications and experience, and how many teachers in the school are certified. But I would be much more interested in knowing how a teacher deals with real life situations than in how many textbook courses she has taken. Does she give a comforting hug to the horrified perpetrator of a crime he "didn't mean" to commit? Does she get down on the child's level to look and listen to him? Does she treat each child with respect while recognizing the needs of the group? Only to such a teacher do you want to entrust your child.

The third area you will want to evaluate will be the physical surroundings. Are the rooms sunny and bright? Do the children have enough space? Is there an outdoor playground? What are the toilet facilities like? Look at the kind, the quality, and the quantity of equipment. It can be enormously expensive or homemade, but it should be sturdy and safe, and lend itself to a variety of uses. As with the teacher, your concern with the physical plant should not be how it looks, but how well it functions for your child. If it's cheerful and pleasant and comfortably disarranged, a school doesn't have to have all the latest educational toys to be good. What it *should* have, however, is an environment that encourages your child to think, to wonder, to try out new solutions, and to have confidence in his ability to figure things out for himself.

You will notice that we have said nothing about paper-and-pencil work, nothing about teaching letters or numbers in the nursery school. At this level, children are not ready for small muscle activities such as writing, or fine perceptual discriminations such as noticing the difference between M and N. They need activities that involve the whole body, an environment that stimulates total learning—physical, social, and emotional as well as intellectual. The best training for reading is learning to put things in order so that the child notices samenesses and differences. Arithmetic begins with one-to-one correspondence (one celery stick for each child, one spoon at each place); from such experiences grow the ideas of number and quantity. Sometimes parents and/or nursery schools try to teach rote material such as the alphabet or the number series which are still meaningless to the child. Their efforts might better be directed toward active kinds of learning such as letting the child figure out for himself that three cupcakes are enough for three children while two are not. The abstract symbol 3 means nothing, while the concrete presence of three cupcakes can make the difference between satisfaction or tragedy!

All through these pages we have pointed out the need for babies to be able to explore and discover and construct the world for themselves. Piaget feels strongly that schools should provide children with the same kinds of opportunities for mental exploration. It is their responsibility to develop minds that are capable of dealing with the unknown world of tomorrow. In Piaget's lifetime the whole world and its technology have changed; Sputnik, the atom bomb, men on the moon, and the explorations of outer space have all revolutionized our view of the universe. Piaget is concerned that our children be ready to meet the challenges of tomorrow. He is afraid that they are too passive in their learn-

ing, that they recite rote answers in school and accept TV commercials at home without critical appraisal. Perhaps his most-quoted statement is the following:

> The principal goal of education is to create men who are capable of doing new things, not simply of repeating what other generations have done—men who are creative, inventive, and discoverers. The second goal of education is to form minds which can be critical, can verify, and not accept everything they are offered. The great danger today is of slogans, collective opinions, ready-made trends of thought. We have to be able to resist individually, to criticize, to distinguish between what is proven and what is not. So we need pupils who are active, who learn early to find out by themselves, partly by their own spontaneous activity and partly through material we set up for them; who learn early to tell what is verifiable and what is simply the first idea to come to them.

This is the kind of education that will prepare your child for an unknown future—and it begins at home. If you want him to venture out into the world unafraid, let him explore and experiment at home. If you want him to question political propaganda or media advertising, encourage him to question and reason at home. Give him the freedom to choose whenever it is appropriate, and to make his own mistakes as long as they are not destructive. This is the quickest and most effective kind of learning. As Piaget points out, children don't learn to swim by sitting on the dock watching the instructor demonstrate. They learn by getting into the water and trying for themselves.

You are your child's first and most important teacher. His future is in your hands. You can help him get into the water.

Outline of Piaget's Periods of Cognitive Development

Sensory-Motor Period (First Two Years)

Stage 1 (Birth to 1 month). The newborn's behavior is character-ized by inborn reflexes (i.e., rooting, sucking, grasping), which become more efficient and combine with each other to form primitive schemas such as rooting-and-sucking. The infant is "locked in egocentrism," with no awareness of self as such or of the distinction between self and the outer world.

Stage 2 (1 to 4 months). The infant begins to define the limits of his own body through accidental discoveries which prove interest-ing. He repeats his movements in order to prolong such experi-ences, combining looking with grasping, for example, to form a more complex organization of behavior called *prehension.*

Stage 3 (4 to 8 months). The baby learns to adapt familiar schemas to new situations, and uses them to "make interesting spectacles last." His interest is focused less on his own body and more on the world about him. He will reach for objects as long as he can see them, but out of sight is out of mind. He uses habitual schemas in a "magical" way, as if he considers his actions capable of causing unrelated external events to happen.

Stage 4 (8 to 12 months). The emergence of intentional behavior is seen as the baby pushes aside obstacles or uses his parent's hand to reach for desired objects. He may search for toys only partly concealed or hidden right before his eyes. He uses familiar schemas in new ways, combining and coordinating them to fit new situations *(mobile schemas).* His anticipatory behavior and his imitation of sounds and actions reveal the beginnings of memory and representation.

Stage 5 (12 to 18 months). The toddler now begins to experiment systematically, varying his schemas in "directed groping." He uses new means such as sticks and strings to attain desired ends, or finds new uses for familiar objects. He is able to follow visible displacements of an object being hidden, and finds it where it was last seen, but cannot infer the results of unseen displacements. He recognizes pictures of familiar persons or objects and can follow simple verbal directions.

Stage 6 (18 to 24 months). This stage marks the transition from sensory-motor activity to mental activity. The toddler invents new means through mental deduction; trial-and-error "groping" is no longer acted out physically but is carried out symbolically or mentally. The child is now able to deduce the invisible displacements of a hidden object; he clearly knows that it continues to exist even when he does not see it. He is beginning to use symbols in language and make-believe play; he remembers past events and imitates them at a later time. He shows purpose, intention, and the beginnings of deductive reasoning, along with a primitive understanding of space, time, and causality. The child is entering the period of symbolic representation.

Preoperational Period (Two to Seven Years)

Preconceptual Stage (2 to 4 years). The child is operating on the level of symbolic representation as evidenced by imitation and memory shown in drawings, dreams, language, and make-believe play. The first overgeneralized attempts at conceptualization appear, in which representatives of a class are not distinguished from the class itself (e.g., all slugs are "the slug").

While the child manages quite realistically in the physical world, his thinking is still egocentric and dominated by a sense of magic omnipotence. He assumes that all natural objects are alive and have feelings and intention because *he* does. He reasons that things which happen coincidentally have a cause-and-effect relationship. He assumes that the world is as it appears to him; he cannot mentally conceive of another person's point of view.

Prelogical or Intuitive Stage (4 to 7 years). Prelogical reasoning appears, based on perceptual appearances (e.g., half a cup of milk which fills a small glass is more than half a cup which doesn't fill a large glass). Trial and error may lead to an intuitive discovery of correct relationships, but the child is unable to take into account more than one attribute at a time (e.g., blue beads cannot at the same time be wooden beads). Language is used in an egocentric way, reflecting the child's limited experience.

Period of Concrete Operations (Seven to Twelve Years)

During the first and second grades there is a gradual transition into the period of *concrete operations,* which lasts until the age of eleven or twelve. The child in this stage can think logically about things he has experienced and manipulate them symbolically, as in arithmetic operations. An extremely important development is that he now is able to think backwards and forwards in time. He recognizes that if half a cup of milk is poured from a tall glass into a short glass, it still must be only half a cup even though it looks like more, because it was only half a cup in the beginning. Piaget calls this ability to reason backwards *reversibility*. It speeds up logical thinking tremendously and makes possible such deductions as "If 2 + 2 equals 4, then 4 − 2 must equal 2."

Here we can see the upward spiraling of intellectual development from the knowledge constructed during the concrete experiences of the sensory-motor period to the ability to represent such experiences symbolically, and finally to think about them abstractly. The elementary school child can put things in series, classify them in groups, and perform other logical operations on them. If you show him a stick A which is longer than a stick B, and then a stick C which is shorter than B, he can deduce that A must logically be longer than C without having to see and compare them on a sensory-motor level.

Period of Formal Operations (Twelve Years to Adulthood)

Somewhere around eleven or twelve the youngster becomes able to reason logically about abstract propositions, things, or properties that he has never directly experienced. This ability to hypothesize characterizes the period of *formal operations*, which is the last and highest period in Piaget's developmental model. The student is capable of deductive and inductive reasoning based on the *form* of a given proposition. His knowledge of the problem may be purely hypothetical, yet he is able to reason it through to a logical conclusion. Examples of such thinking include problems in mathematics or chemistry or experiments which manipulate a number of variables in a systematic and all-inclusive manner. Not all adults fully achieve this last and highest stage of intellectual development, but certainly such thinking is characteristic of scientists and researchers who work with atoms, quarks, and nuclear fission. Such thinkers are able to cut through masses of material and come up with a clear, encompassing explanation. As Einstein is reputed to have said of Piaget's theory, "It is so simple that only a genius could have thought of it."

Suggestions for Further Reading

Child Development and Child Care

Brazelton, T. Berry. *Infants and Mothers: Differences in Development.* New York: Dell, 1972.

———. *Toddlers and Parents: A Declaration of Independence.* New York: Dell, 1976.

Bruner, Jerome; Cole, Michael; and Lloyd, Barbara, eds. *The Developing Child Series.* Cambridge, Mass.: Harvard Univ. Press, 1977. Includes Aidan Macfarlane, "The Psychology of Childbirth"; Rudolph Schaffer, "Mothering"; Judy Dunn, "Distress and Comfort"; Catherine Garvey, "Play."

Caplan, Frank, ed. *The First Twelve Months of Life: Your Baby's Growth Month by Month.* New York: Grosset & Dunlap, 1973.

Church, Joseph, ed. *Three Babies: Biographies of Cognitive Development.* New York: Random House, 1966.

———. *Understanding Your Child From Birth to Three: A Guide to Your Child's Psychological Development.* New York: Random House, 1973.

Fraiberg, Selma H. *The Magic Years: Understanding and Handling the*

Problems of Early Childhood. New York: Scribner's, 1959.

————. *Every Child's Birthright: In Defense of Mothering.* New York: Basic Books, 1977.

Piaget, Jean. *The Child's Conception of the World.* Totowa, N.J.: Littlefield, Adams & Co., 1965.

————. *The Construction of Reality in the Child.* New York: Basic Books, 1954.

————. *The Origins of Intelligence in Children.* New York: W. W. Norton, 1963.

————. *Play, Dreams and Imitation in Childhood.* New York: W. W. Norton, 1962.

Pulaski, Mary Ann. *Understanding Piaget: An Introduction to Children's Cognitive Development.* New York: Harper & Row, 1971.

White, Burton L. *The First Three Years of Life.* Englewood Cliffs, N.J.: Prentice-Hall, 1975.

Play and Activities

Kelly, Marguerite, and Parsons, Elia. *The Mother's Almanac: Loving and Living with Small Children.* New York: Doubleday, 1975.

Lehane, Stephen. *Help Your Baby Learn: 100 Piaget-Based Activities for the First Two Years of Life.* Englewood Cliffs, N.J.: Prentice-Hall, 1976.

Marzollo, Jean, and Lloyd, Janet. *Learning Through Play.* New York: Harper & Row, 1972.

Singer, Dorothy G., and Singer, Jerome L. *Partners in Play: A Step-by-Step Guide to Imaginative Play in Children.* New York: Harper & Row, 1977.

Conception and Birth

Holland, Vikki. *We Are Having a Baby.* New York: Scribner's, 1972.

Sheffield, Margaret. *Where Do Babies Come From?* New York: Knopf, 1972.

Stein, Sara Bonnett. *Making Babies.* New York: Walker & Co., 1974.

————. *That New Baby.* New York: Walker & Co., 1974.

Play Groups, Nursery Schools, and Day Care

Curtis, Jean. *A Parents' Guide to Nursery Schools.* New York: Random House, 1971.

―――. *Working Mothers.* Garden City, N.Y.: Doubleday, 1976.

Evans, E. Belle, and Saia, George E. *Day Care for Infants: The Case for Infant Day Care and a Practical Guide.* Boston: Beacon Press, 1972.

Hymes, James L., Jr. *Teaching the Child Under Six.* Columbus, Ohio: Merrill, 1968.

Olds, Sally W. *The Mother Who Works Outside the Home.* New York: Child Study Press, 1975.

Pitcher, Evelyn G., and Ames, Louise B. *The Guidance Nursery School.* Rev. ed. New York: Harper & Row, 1975.

Winn, Marie, and Porcher, Mary Ann. *The Playgroup Book.* New York: Macmillan, 1967.

Notes

Introduction

Page 4. Published in French in 1936; English translation now available in paperback (New York: W. W. Norton, 1963).

Page 6. Eleanor Duckworth, "Piaget Takes a Teacher's Look," *Learning* 2, no. 2 (October 1963): 25.

Page 8. Margaret Mahler, Fred Pine, and Anni Bergman, *The Psychological Birth of the Human Infant* (New York: Basic Books, 1975), p. 3.

Page 10. United States Department of Labor, Women's Bureau, *Working Mothers and Their Children* (Washington, D.C.: U.S. Government Printing Office, 1977), p. 1f.

Chapter 1

Page 19. Aidan Macfarlane, *The Psychology of Childbirth* (Cambridge, Mass.: Harvard Univ. Press, 1977), esp. chap. 6.

Pages 20–21. Peter H. Wolff, "Observations on the Early Development of Smiling," in L. Joseph Stone, Henrietta T. Smith, and Lois B. Murphy, eds., *The Competent Infant* (New York: Basic Books, 1973), pp. 1070–1081.

Page 21. E. R. John et al., "Neurometrics," *Science* 196, no. 4297 (24 June 1977):1393–409.

Page 24. Lee Salk, quoted in Macfarlane, *Psychology of Childbirth*, p. 9.

Chapter 2

Page 29. Jean Piaget, *The Origins of Intelligence in Children* (New York: W. W. Norton, 1963) p. 52.

Page 30. *Ibid.*, p. 96.

Page 32. *Ibid.*, p. 111.

Page 34. Burton L. White, "The Initial coordination of Sensorimotor Schemas in Human Infants," in David Elkind and John Flavell, eds., *Studies in Cognitive Development* (New York: Oxford Univ. Press, 1969), p. 238.

Page 35. E. R. Siqueland, quoted in Stone et al., eds., *Competent Infant*, p. 456.

Page 36. Burton White, "Child Development Research," in *ibid.*, pp. 812–21.

Page 38. Mahler et al., *Psychological Birth of the Human Infant*, p. 44.

Chapter 3

Page 47. Piaget, *Origins of Intelligence*, p. 159.

Page 49. *Ibid.*, p. 185.

Page 50. Jean Piaget, *The Construction of Reality in the Child* (New York: Basic Books, 1954), pp. 19–20.

Page 52. *Ibid.*, p. 21.

Page 53. William Kessen and Katherine Nelson, quoted in *Carnegie Quarterly* 24, no. 2 (Spring 1976): 1.

Page 58. Milton Kotelchuck, "The Infant's Relationship to the Father: Experimental Evidence," in Michael E. Lamb, ed., *The Role of the Father in Child Development* (New York: Wiley, 1976), pp. 329–43.

Chapter 4

Page 65. Piaget, *Origins of Intelligence*, p. 215.

Page 66. *Ibid.*, p. 256.

Page 66. *Ibid.*, p. 223.

Page 68. *Ibid.*, p. 217.

Page 69. Piaget, *Construction of Reality*, p. 52.

Page 70. *Ibid.*, p. 62.

Page 74. Michael E. Lamb, "Interactions Between Eight-Month-Old Children and Their Fathers and Mothers," in Lamb, ed., *Role of the Father in Child Development*, pp. 307–25.

Page 78. For some of these ideas I am deeply indebted to Dr. Judith Kestenberg, who shared with me her unpublished papers on this subject briefly touched upon in her book *Children and Parents* (New York: Jason Aronson, 1975) and developed more fully in Judith Kestenberg and Joan Weinstein, "Transitional Objects and Body Image Formation," in Simon Grolnick and Leonard Barken, eds., *Between Reality and Fantasy: Transitional Objects and Phenomena* (New York: Jason Arenson, 1978), pp. 75–95.

Page 80. Burton L. White, *The First Three Years of Life* (Englewood Cliffs, N.J.: Prentice-Hall, 1975), pp. 129–30.

Chapter 5

Page 85. Selma Fraiberg, *The Magic Years* (New York: Scribner's, 1959), p. 60.

Page 86. Phyllis Greenacre, quoted by Mahler in *Psychological Birth of the Human Infant*, p. 70.

Page 88. Piaget, *Origins of Intelligence*, p. 283.

Page 90. *Ibid.*, p. 301.

Page 91. Piaget, *Construction of Reality*, p. 67.

Page 92. *Ibid.*, p. 68.

Page 93. *Ibid.*, p. 73.

Page 95. See Thérèse Gouin Décarie, *Intelligence and Affectivity in Early Childhood* (New York: International Univ. Press, 1965), esp. pp. 25 ff. and 212.

Page 96. Ernst Abelin, "The Role of the Father in the Separation-Individuation Process," in J. B. McDevitt and C. F. Settlage, eds., *Separation-Individuation* (New York: International Univ. Press, 1971), p. 239.

Chapter 6

Page 105. Piaget, *Construction of Reality,* p. 81.

Page 106. Jean Piaget, *Play, Dreams and Imitation in Childhood* (New York: W. W. Norton, 1962), p. 63.

Page 106. T. Berry Brazelton, *Toddlers and Parents* (New York: Delacorte Press/Seymour Lawrence, 1974), p. 59.

Page 106. Ina Uzgiris, "Patterns of Vocal and Gestural Imitation in Infants," in Stone et al., eds., *Competent Infant,* pp. 599–604.

Page 108. Nathan Isaacs, quoted in Mildred Hardeman, ed., *Children's Ways of Knowing* (New York: Teachers College Press, 1974) p. 136.

Page 112. John Bowlby, *Separation, Anxiety, and Anger* (New York: Basic Books, 1973).

Chapter 7

Page 124. Piaget, *Play, Dreams and Imitation,* p. 258.

Page 125. Wayne Dennis, "Piaget's Questions Applied to a Child of Known Environment," *Journal of Genetic Psychology* 60 (1942): 307–20.

Page 125. Piaget, *Play, Dreams and Imitation,* pp. 250–52.

Page 128. Jean Piaget, *The Child's Conception of the World* (Totowa, N.J.: Littlefield, Adams & Co., 1965), p. 92ff.

Page 130. *Ibid.,* pp. 76ff.

Page 131. Piaget, *Play, Dreams and Imitation,* p. 235.

Page 132. *Ibid.,* p. 225.

Page 132. Examples from Piaget's *Play, Dreams and Imitation* and *Child's Conception of the World.*

Chapter 8

Pages 144–47. Jean Piaget, *The Moral Judgment of the Child* (New York: Free Press, 1965), p. 24.

Page 149. Joseph Church, ed., *Three Babies: Biographies of Cognitive Development* (New York: Random House, 1966), p. 24.

Page 150. Piaget, *Play, Dreams and Imitation,* p. 125.

Page 151. *Ibid.,* p. 133.

Page 153. *Ibid.,* p. 168.

Page 154. *Ibid.*, p. 289.

Pages 154–55. Dorothy G. Singer and Jerome L. Singer, *Partners in Play* (New York: Harper & Row, 1977), p. 10.

Chapter 9

Page 158. Wolff, "The Natural History of Crying and Other Vocalizations in Early Infancy," in Stone et al., eds., *Competent Infant*, pp. 1185–97.

Page 160. M. M. Lewis, *How Children Learn to Speak* (New York: Basic Books, 1959), pp. 79–88.

Page 166. Roger Brown, *A First Language* (Cambridge, Mass.: Harvard Univ. Press, 1973), p. 249.

Page 168. Examples taken from Kornei Chukovsky, *From Two to Five* (Berkeley: Univ. of California Press, 1971).

Page 169. The words of Colin, a three-and-one-half-year-old boy quoted by Lois Murphy in *Personality in Young Children*, 2 (New York: Basic Books, 1956): 263.

Chapter 10

Page 171. Anne C. Bernstein and Philip A. Cowan, "Children's Concepts of How People Get Babies," *Child Development* 46 (1975): 77–91.

Page 176. Selma Fraiberg, *Every Child's Birthright: In Defense of Mothering* (New York: Basic Books, 1977), p. 86.

Page 184. Richard E. Ripple and Verne O. Rockcastle, eds., *Piaget Rediscovered: A Report of the Conference on Cognitive Studies and Curriculum Development*, School of Education, Cornell University, March 1964, p. 5.

Index

About the Author

Mary Ann Spencer Pulaski was born in New York City and grew up in Fukuoka, Japan, where her parents were Methodist missionaries. She married soon after graduating from Wellesley College, and worked at various jobs while raising her two children. When they were grown, she returned to graduate study at Queens College and the City University of New York, where she received her Ph.D. in psychology in 1968.

Dr. Pulaski has taught elementary school classes and college students, has lectured extensively on child development, and has been school psychologist for the Herricks (Long Island) Public Schools since 1967. She has served as president of the Nassau County Psychological Association, and was elected a Fellow of the American Psychological Association. She now serves on the International Advisory Board of the Jean Piaget Society, after several years as a member of its Executive Board. Among her published works is *Understanding Piaget: An Introduction to Children's Cognitive Development*, published by Harper & Row in 1971.

Photo Credits